Chemistry, Faith, and Stewardship

Chemistry, Faith, and Stewardship

Uniting Biblical Wisdom with Scientific Practice

LIZA ABRAHAM

FOREWORD BY
Sy Garte

RESOURCE *Publications* • Eugene, Oregon

CHEMISTRY, FAITH, AND STEWARDSHIP
Uniting Biblical Wisdom with Scientific Practice

Copyright © 2025 Liza Abraham. All rights reserved. Except for brief quotations in critical publications or reviews, no part of this book may be reproduced in any manner without prior written permission from the publisher. Write: Permissions, Wipf and Stock Publishers, 199 W. 8th Ave., Suite 3, Eugene, OR 97401.

Resource Publications
An Imprint of Wipf and Stock Publishers
199 W. 8th Ave., Suite 3
Eugene, OR 97401

www.wipfandstock.com

PAPERBACK ISBN: 979-8-3852-5805-5
HARDCOVER ISBN: 979-8-3852-5806-2
EBOOK ISBN: 979-8-3852-5807-9

10/09/25

Scripture quotations are taken from the *Holy Bible*, New International Version® (NIV®). Copyright © 1973, 1978, 1984, 2011 by Biblica, Inc.™ Used by permission. All rights reserved worldwide.

To God, the source of all knowledge and wisdom, and to my father, who gifted me my first Bible at the age of nine, and to students who seek to love Him and stand firmly on His Word, even as they explore the wonders of science.

"On that day you will realize that I am in my Father, and you are in me, and I am in you. Whoever has my commands and keeps them is the one who loves me. The one who loves me will be loved by my Father, and I too will love them and show myself to them."

— John 14:20-21 (NIV)

Contents

Foreword by Sy Garte		ix
Preface		xiii
Acknowledgments		xv
Introduction		xvii
1	The Earth: A Realm of God's Glory and Reign	1
2	Rooted and Flourishing: The Story of Trees in Scripture and Nature	15
3	Living Water: The Flow of God's Life	27
4	Precious Stones: God's Transformation Work to Form His House	37
5	Light and Matter: Interaction that Reveals Life	47
6	The Rhythm of Rest: Sabbath and the Whisper of God	56
7	A Man According to God's Heart : Delighting in God and His Word	68
8	Building on the Rock: A Life Anchored in the Word	80
9	Chemistry: The Central Science Revealing Divine Design	91
10	Stewardship in Chemistry: Guiding the Next Generation of Innovators	101

Contents

11 The Spiritual Man: Living with the Mind of Christ   111
Bibliography   121

Foreword

A CRITICAL ISSUE FOR our world today is the relationship between science and faith. Once known to be in beautiful harmony, the rise of scientific atheism in the late 19th century led to the promulgation of a false doctrine of a basic conflict between the world of nature, as described by science, and any kind of Biblical, religious or faith-based world view.

Many books have been written showing the falsity of this conflict thesis, reflecting the reality of the origin of all the modern sciences among deeply religious Christian philosophers and experimentalists. As more and more scientific truths about the structure and function of the natural world were revealed through scientific methods, pioneers like Newton, Boyle, Pasteur, Faraday, Maxwell, Kelvin and so many others rejoiced in the revelations that fulfilled, rather than opposed biblical and theological ideology.

And yet, today we see the legacy of decades of anti-religious bias in academia, the media, and throughout our culture, especially in intellectual, educational and influential circles. The rise of "new atheism" in the early 2000s led to an explosive growth in the number of young people who neither cared nor knew anything about God or religion – the rise of the "nones."

More recently, the intellectual and scientific basis for the new atheist ideology has begun to crumble under the weight of its contradictions and denials of obvious truths. The famous Dawkins quote about living in a universe entirely devoid of purpose, meaning, design, good or evil, has been recognized as false, and the attempt to convert everyone to the irrational philosophy of pure materialism is losing ground rapidly.

This book by Liza Abraham is a valuable contribution to the ongoing struggle by Christian academics and scientists to help reverse the trend toward deconversion and ultimate loss of faith among the young and disillusioned. Beautifully written from a strong biblical viewpoint, Abraham skillfully weaves scriptural teachings with natural wonders to present a holistic picture of our world that is totally consistent with a divine creator and the salvation of Jesus Christ.

While much of the material is poetic and spiritual in tone, each chapter includes very practical and valuable sections for hands on experience in simple chemical and biological laboratory work, relevant to the subject matter discussed in the chapter. There are also a set of questions for readers and students to ponder and answer at the end of each chapter, making this book a valuable resource in an educational setting.

The author's point of view is infused with a strong theme of creation care, and environmental concern, which will make the book attractive to students with an environmentally aware consciousness. She very gracefully blends a great deal of chemical and biological knowledge into her overall theological and non-technical descriptions of our wondrous natural world. The result is an enormously valuable educational tool for students of Christian faith.

Each chapter is devoted to a specific theme from the world of nature, and/or the word of Scripture. These include trees, water, stones and the fundamental nature of matter and light, as components of the natural word. The chapter on water for example explores the multitude of ways that water chemistry contributes to the miracle of life, which is then related to the importance of water in the bible. I was especially delighted with the section in Chapter 5 on the dual nature of light as both a wave and a particle, in relation to the dual nature of Christ as both human and divine. This is a theme I have included in my own writing.

Foreword

The author also provides the reader with two excellent chapters about her main scientific love – chemistry. This one quote illustrates the spiritually poetic, yet scientifically accurate tone of the book: "Water does more than hydrate; it nurtures. Carbon does more than bond; it builds."

The four chapters on biblical theology exhibit a masterful portrayal of the beautiful harmony between science and biblical faith. Abraham includes examples of faithful Christian scientists, including Alister McGrath (who wrote the foreword for my first book). She covers a great deal of ground with biblical exegesis, including how the Old and New Testaments should encourage our faith and lead us in the light of Christ.

To sum up, this book is educational, inspirational, rational, biblical, and thoroughly enjoyable. And it will be a marvelous witness to the truth of both God's world as revealed by modern science and of God's word in scripture. Enjoy it, and God bless.

Sy Garte

Preface

SINCE 2015, TEACHING AT Christian institutions, I have encountered students at many different stages in their faith journey. Some have never cultivated a personal relationship with Jesus; others attend church regularly. Some read the Bible occasionally, while others engage with it often. Many have never shared their faith with friends. My burden as an educator is to shepherd students toward cultivating a personal relationship with the Lord—to develop a taste for the Bible, not merely reading it, but engaging with it prayerfully and spending personal time with Him.

In my classroom, I have seen students struggle to reconcile their Christian faith with their scientific studies. Some are unsure whether it is possible to love God fully while embracing disciplines like chemistry, biology, or engineering. This tension inspired me to write this book: to provide a resource that encourages students to see science and faith not as opposing forces, but as complementary avenues for understanding God's creation.

This book is intended to guide students of faith in higher education, helping them to integrate their academic pursuits with a vibrant spiritual life. It is also written for a broader audience, including educators and parents, who wish to encourage the next generation to pursue knowledge while remaining firmly rooted in Scripture. My hope is that readers will be equipped to approach learning with intellectual curiosity and spiritual discernment, cultivating both a love for God and a passion for discovery.

Acknowledgments

I AM GRATEFUL TO Dr. Sy Garte for graciously writing the foreword to this book. His thoughtful contribution and kind support are both an honor and an encouragement to me. This book has grown out of my experiences with young people and the many conversations I have shared with them. In countless ways, they have shaped this work, often without realizing it. From my time with them, I witnessed the twinkle in their eyes, their growing love for the Lord and the Scriptures, and their sincere questions about life, faith, and science. Their curiosity, struggles, and joys have been a constant reminder of the responsibility and privilege of guiding the next generation in both academic and spiritual growth.

The discipline of chemistry, by its nature, is both divine and mysterious. Its principles, patterns, and metaphors often reflect the ways the Lord reveals truth and invite us to explore the depths of the divine-human relationship. When approached with a mind open to both science and faith, chemistry becomes more than a study of matter. It becomes a lens through which we encounter God's creativity and wisdom. Veils are lifted, scales fall from our eyes, and the ears of our hearts are anointed. Chemistry becomes a journey with the Creator, an opportunity to uncover the precious truths embedded in His creation and to marvel at the intricacy of His design.

I am deeply grateful for the fellowship and encouragement I have received within my faith community. Their prayers, guidance, and shared love for the Scriptures have nourished my own spiritual journey and, in turn, this book. To all who have prayed, listened, asked thoughtful questions, and walked alongside me, this work is as much yours as it is mine. I am especially thankful to Carol Sorrels, who sent notes of encouragement and prayed with me throughout the writing of this book.

Introduction

THIS BOOK IS AN invitation to anchor your mind and heart in God, to love Him with all your being, and to delight in His Word. It calls you to see science not as separate from your faith but as a lens through which God's wisdom, creativity, and care are revealed. Every discovery in the laboratory, every observation in nature, can become an opportunity to glorify the Creator and grow in understanding of His truth.

The journey begins with the earth itself, and the ways it reflects God's glory and care. From there, it moves through the life of trees, the flow of water, and the transformative power found in God's design, touching on light, matter, and the rhythms of rest that sustain both creation and our souls. Along the way, the chapters draw connections between Scripture and science, revealing how God shapes His world and invites us into thoughtful stewardship. Later sections reflect on the spiritual life, showing how the mind of Christ can guide our actions, our study, and our service, including our work in chemistry and the broader sciences.

Each chapter is designed to be both instructive and reflective. Hands-on activities engage scientific principles while Scripture passages provide a lens for spiritual insight. Following each activity, five reflection questions encourage meditation, ethical consideration, and personal growth. These exercises cultivate discernment, character, and a deeper awareness of God's presence in the learning process.

INTRODUCTION

Written primarily for students of faith, this book is also for educators, parents, and anyone seeking to integrate intellectual pursuit with spiritual formation. My hope is that you will see chemistry not merely as a subject to master, but as a calling to explore, serve, and care for creation wisely. Approach each activity with curiosity, each reflection with honesty, and each discovery with awe. In doing so, you will not only learn more about God's creation—you will come to know more of the God who sustains it and the role you are called to play in His ongoing work.

I

The Earth
A Realm of God's Glory and Reign

EARTH AS THE STAGE OF GOD'S GLORY

"The earth is the Lord's, and everything in it" (Ps 24:1a). This profound truth anchors our understanding of the world: the land beneath our feet, the oceans, the creatures, the air we breathe, and the resources we rely on all belong to God. The earth is not a random planet drifting through space, but a purposeful creation where God reveals his glory, exercises his authority, and invites humanity into relationship.

The prophet Zechariah paints a sweeping picture of God's creative work: "The LORD, who stretches out the heavens, who lays the foundation of the earth, and who forms the human spirit within a person" (Zech 12:1). From the vastness of the heavens to the intimate formation of the human spirit, each element reveals deliberate design and purpose. The heavens declare God's majesty (Ps 19:1; Ps 8 3–4; Isa 40:26; Neh 9:6), and the earth serves as our home and the setting for his unfolding plan (Gen 1:28; Ps 104:24; Isa 45:18). Most intimately, God shapes the human spirit, inviting us into a personal relationship with him (Prov 20:27; Ezek 36:26; Ps 51:10; 1 Cor 6:17; 1 Cor 2:11; Rom 1:9; 2 Tim 4:22; 1 Pet 3:4; Heb 4:12; 1 Thess 5:23). God not only shaped the universe, but also formed the core of who we are, so that we might love him, know him, and be filled with his presence (Isa 54:5a, Jer 2:2, Exod 33:13, Jer 9:24, Isa 11:9, Eph 3:16–19, Col 2:9–10, Gal 2:20, 2 Cor 3:18).

This longing for relationship is powerfully echoed in Isaiah 66:1–2, where God says, "Heaven is my throne, and the earth is my footstool . . . These are the ones I look on with favor: those who are humble and contrite in spirit, and who tremble at my word." God isn't looking for impressive buildings or rituals; he's looking for open, humble hearts. He desires to dwell with people who revere his word and open their spirits to him. His ultimate resting place is not temples made by human hands, but the whole person—spirit, soul, and body—sanctified and kept blameless for his presence and purpose (1 Thess 5:23).

Paul writes, "In him the whole building is joined together and rises to become a holy temple in the LORD. And in him you too are being built together to become a dwelling in which God lives by his Spirit" (Eph 2:21–22). Like newborn infants, we are to long for the pure, guileless milk of the word so that by it we may grow unto salvation. Christ is the living Stone, and as we come to him, we also become living stones, fitted and joined together to form a spiritual house, a holy temple where God dwells by his Spirit (1 Pet 2:2–5).

We are not the masters of the earth, nor are we called to idolize, exploit, or dismiss it. Instead, we are stewards, entrusted by God with the land, its creatures, and its resources—not as owners, but as caretakers (Gen 2:15; Ps 115:16; Ps 8:6–8). The earth is not merely our dwelling place; it is the sacred setting where God reveals his glory and declares the majesty of his name (Ps 8:1, 9). When we live as faithful stewards, redeemed by grace, attentive to his word, and aligned with his purpose, the earth becomes more than a backdrop for human activity. It becomes a living stage where the glory of God is made known.

Psalm 24 opens with a powerful affirmation that the earth and all it contains belong to the LORD. It concludes with a majestic image of the King of Glory entering in. This vision of the earth as a sacred and meaningful space brings us back to the beginning, when God first created humanity with intention and entrusted them with the care of his creation. As Isaiah 6:3b proclaims, "The whole earth is full of his glory."

GOD'S ORIGINAL DESIGN AND OUR LOST STEWARDSHIP

From the very beginning, God created the earth with intention, to reflect his glory and serve as a vessel of his authority. Genesis 1:27-28 reveals this divine purpose: "God created mankind in his own image... and said, 'Be fruitful and increase in number; fill the earth and subdue it." Humanity was entrusted with dominion, not to exploit or dominate, but to reflect God's heart and reign through wisdom, love, and responsible care.

Yet this design was disrupted. In Genesis 3, Satan deceived Adam and Eve, introducing sin, rebellion, and death into the world. Humanity's fellowship with God was broken, and their role as stewards of the earth was compromised. As a result, creation itself was subjected to corruption and now groans in longing for restoration, awaiting the day when it will be brought into the freedom and glory of the children of God (Rom 8:20—22). The earth, once a place of harmony and communion, became marked by toil, thorns, and estrangement.

Yet God did not abandon his original plan for the earth. He called Abraham (Gen 12:1-3), choosing to form a covenant people through whom blessing would extend to all nations. Israel was to be a kingdom of priests (Exod 19:6), a living testimony of God's justice, mercy, and holiness. So that through their life and worship, the nations might see what it looks like when God reigns among his people on the earth he created for his glory.

Though Israel often failed to reflect God's reign, leading to exile and judgment, God's covenant love never failed. Through the prophets, he foretold a restoration far beyond national borders: Isaiah 9:6-7 foretells the coming of a child who would reign "with justice and righteousness from that time on and forever." This promise pointed forward to Jesus Christ, in whom all the fullness of the Godhead lives in bodily form (Col 2:9).

Jesus came proclaiming, "The kingdom of God is at hand" (Mark 1:15). But this kingdom did not arrive through force or political power; it unfolded through acts of compassion: healing the sick, feeding the hungry, welcoming the outcast, and ultimately laying down his life in love. Through his death and resurrection, Christ broke the curse of sin, triumphed over death, and reclaimed the authority that had been forfeited. "All authority in heaven and on earth has been given to me," he declared (Matt 28:18). In him, God's original design is already being restored, first in humanity and ultimately in all creation, until the day his renewal is fully complete. As his kingdom takes root in us, we are made new—a transformed creation—shaped by his life within and no longer defined by what we were. This inward renewal is what truly matters, and it prepares us for the day of his return, when a new heaven and a new earth will fully reflect his glory (1 Thess 5:23).

Now, as redeemed people living on this earth, we are invited to participate in this renewal. In Christ, we are being restored to our true vocation: to bear God's image, steward the earth with reverence, and reflect his character through lives marked by humility, justice, and love.

WHEN CREATION SPEAKS: SCIENTIFIC ECHOES OF GOD'S DESIGN

The earth is not silent. Scripture reveals that the land, seas, skies, and living creatures do more than merely exist, they proclaim God's glory, reflect his beauty, and participate in his purposes. Psalm 96:11–12 calls all creation to rejoice:

> "Let the heavens rejoice, let the earth be glad . . . let the fields be jubilant . . . let all the trees of the forest sing for joy."

The Earth

This poetic imagery communicates a profound truth: creation itself responds to and honors its Creator. Similarly, Isaiah 55:12 uses vivid language to describe the natural world as alive with praise:

"The mountains and hills will burst into song before you, and all the trees of the field will clap their hands."

While figurative, these expressions affirm that the earth's fruitfulness, harmony, and beauty serve as a witness to God's glory. This biblical testimony finds a parallel in scientific observation. The intricate patterns of the earth, the changing seasons, the balance of ecosystems, and the complex interdependence of living organisms, demonstrate a level of design, care, and purpose that aligns with the notion of divine wisdom sustaining all things. Isaiah 45:12 declares:

"I have made the earth . . . My own hands stretched out the heavens." Colossians 1:17 affirms: "In him all things hold together."

These assertions anticipate the precision and order evident in the natural world, which were described centuries before the advent of modern astronomy and ecology. For instance, biblical texts describe the earth as being "suspended over nothing" (Job 26:7), and God sits enthroned "above the circle of the earth" (Isa 40:22). Phenomena such as the sun's predictable movements (Isa 38:8; Eccl 1:5) and celestial constellations (Job 38:31) are also referenced. Contemporary astronomy has revealed that even the seemingly fixed stars in Orion's Belt gradually shift over time, an observation made possible through precise data from sources such as the Gaia space telescope[1]. These discoveries reflect an ever-unfolding universe consistent with the biblical portrayal of ordered creation.

Similarly, Scripture's references to the ocean and its depths (Gen 7:11; Job 38:16; 2 Sam 22:16) align with modern discoveries such as hydrothermal vents, which support previously unknown ecosystems[2]. Inspired by Psalm 8:8's reference to the "paths

---

1. NASA, *Discovering the Universe*.
2. Lubofsky, *Discovery of Hydrothermal Vents*.

of the seas," Matthew Maury, known as the "father of modern oceanography," pioneered the scientific mapping of ocean currents, demonstrating a tangible bridge between Scripture and science.[3]

Descriptions of atmospheric phenomena and the water cycle are also found in the Old Testament (Job 26:8; Job 36:27–28; Eccl 1:6), highlighting an early understanding of processes vital to sustaining life on earth, processes still studied rigorously today.

The Old Testament authors, then, offer a vision of a world characterized by order, purpose, and praise, an understanding that continues to be affirmed by scientific exploration. Isaiah 45:18 underscores this truth:

"He did not create the earth to be empty, but formed it to be inhabited (Isa 45:18)." Through its intrinsic beauty, structured order, and ongoing responsiveness, the earth magnifies its Maker. Alongside humanity, all creation eagerly awaits the future renewal described in Revelation 21:1:

"Then I saw a new heaven and a new earth . . . " Even now, creation proclaims the glory of God, inviting attentive hearts to listen, care, and join in its eternal praise.

PARABLES FROM NATURE: EVERYDAY WONDERS THAT REVEAL THE CREATOR

After beholding the grandeur of the heavens and the earth—resounding with joy and filled with God's glory, we turn our attention to something smaller, quieter, and closer to home. Yet even in this simple, familiar object lies profound wonder. Consider, for example, the egg.

Though common, inexpensive, and accessible to all, the egg is anything but ordinary. It is a marvel of design, inviting both delight and discovery. Its calcium carbonate shell, delicately formed yet strong, protects the developing life inside. Each part, the yolk, the white, the membranes, and even the tiny air pocket, serves a

---

3. USS Maury AGS-16, *Matthew Fontaine Maury*.

distinct purpose, making the egg a subject of scientific fascination in chemistry, biology, and biochemistry.

The shell is sturdy yet breathable, porous enough to allow air and moisture in to sustain the growing chick. Inside, the yolk provides nourishment, while the white cushions and protects. Even the thin cords that anchor the yolk in place are perfectly designed. Nothing is wasted. Such intricate detail invites not only wonder, but reverence for the One who made it.

From God's perspective, the egg symbolizes nourishment and the promise of new beginnings. To us, it is both food and a subject of scientific research. As we explore its structure, uncovering the harmony of proteins, fats, vitamins, and minerals, we gain a clearer view of how every component functions together with purpose and precision. Scientific exploration, far from being merely academic, becomes a journey into the mind of the Life-Giver. It invites us to pause and marvel, drawing our hearts upward in awe, praise, and worship of the One who sustains all life.

FIRSTFRUITS AND THE FULFILLMENT OF GOD'S KINGDOM

In the Old Testament, God describes the land he is giving to his people, a land abundant with brooks, wheat, vines, fig trees, and more (Deut 8:7, 10). This land was not merely for survival or indulgence, but a place where life could flourish in fellowship with him. Later, he commands, "Take some of the first of all the fruit of the ground . . . " and go to the place where the LORD your God will choose to cause his name to dwell" (Deut 26:2). Throughout the Old Testament, offering the first and best of the harvest (Exod 23:19; Neh 10:35) was a declaration that everything belongs to the LORD and that his satisfaction comes first.

This practice finds its ultimate fulfillment in Christ, "the firstfruits of those who have fallen asleep" (1 Cor 15:20). Jesus is not only the first to rise from the dead, but also the divine seed planted within us. He is both the offering and the indwelling life, the beginning of a new and eternal harvest. As Paul writes, "Not only the creation, but we ourselves, who have the firstfruits of the Spirit, groan inwardly as we wait eagerly for adoption as sons, the redemption of our bodies" (Rom 8:23). Likewise, Revelation affirms, "These have been redeemed from mankind as firstfruits for God and the Lamb" (Rev 14:4).

Christ is the firstfruit, and by abiding in him as branches in the vine, we too become firstfruits, set apart for God, filled with his Spirit, and offered back to him for his pleasure. Even in this imagery, we are reminded in a physical way to care for the earth. God created the earth to be the realm of life, both physical and spiritual. Just as the land was to yield fruit for his dwelling and delight, our lives, rooted in Christ, become the field in which God's eternal purpose is fulfilled. When aligned with God's intention, life on earth becomes the vessel for his kingdom, his presence, and his glory.

SHADOWS THAT POINT TO CHRIST

The earth is filled with images that whisper the name of Christ. The offerings, festivals, and priesthood of the Old Testament served as shadows, preparing hearts for the reality revealed in Jesus. As Colossians 2:16–17 reminds us:

> "Therefore do not let anyone judge you by what you eat or drink, or with regard to a religious festival, a New Moon celebration or a Sabbath day. These are a shadow of the things that were to come; the reality, however, is found in Christ."

Even the animals woven throughout Scripture become living parables that reveal facets of his nature, work, and glory. As the Lamb, Jesus offered himself as the perfect sacrifice, shedding his blood to redeem and reconcile us to God. As the Lion, he rose victorious, reigning in majesty and securing our eternal triumph. And as the Eagle, he lifts us up in the power of his resurrection, teaching us to depend on grace rather than striving. "You yourselves have seen what I did to Egypt, and how I carried you on eagles' wings and brought you to myself" (Exod 19:4). The eagle, soaring high above the earth with unmatched strength and vision, gives wings to his resurrection power, lifting us beyond our human limitations (Phil 3:10; Phil 4:13). Unlike smaller birds that exhaust themselves with constant flapping, eagles flap their wings only briefly. Most of the time, they soar, riding invisible wind currents that lift them effortlessly to great heights. In this, the eagle becomes a living parable of how God sustains us: not by striving, but by trust. "But those who wait for the LORD shall renew their strength; they shall mount up with wings like eagles" (Isa 40:31). This Old Testament image finds its New Testament fulfillment in the sufficiency of grace: "My grace is sufficient for you, for My power is perfected in weakness . . . that the power of Christ may rest [tabernacle] upon me" (2 Cor 12:9). The eagle shows us how God's strength becomes ours when we stop striving and start depending, when we learn to ride the unseen currents of his grace.

THE STORY OF BALD EAGLE

The bald eagle — long a symbol of strength and freedom — was nearly wiped out in the 20th century due to the pesticide DDT. Researchers found that 47 percent of bald eagles and 46 percent of golden eagles showed signs of chronic lead poisoning, buildup from repeated exposure, and as many as 35 percent had acute poisoning from dangerously high lead levels.[4] These sobering statistics call us to action. Bald eagles now face not only lead poisoning, but habitat loss, wind turbine collisions, and entanglement in discarded fishing line. Their continued survival depends not only on policy but also on people: on our willingness to adapt, advocate, and care. Stewardship of creation is not peripheral to faith; it's a reflection of the Creator's own care. As those who follow the Lamb, trust the Lion, and soar with the Eagle, we are called to do the same.

---

4. American Eagle Foundation, *Top Threats to Bald Eagles*.

CHEMISTRY, FAITH, AND STEWARDSHIP

THE STORY OF SALMON RUN

Another living parable of stewardship is found in the salmon run, a remarkable, God-ordained journey that many students have never heard of. Pacific salmon are born in freshwater streams, migrate to the ocean for most of their adult lives, and then, guided by an extraordinary sense of direction, return upstream to the very waters where they were born, to spawn and die. This cycle sustains not only future generations of salmon but also entire ecosystems, providing nutrients to forests, bears, birds, and humans alike. Yet today, the salmon run is under threat. One of the top dangers is water pollution[5]. Industrial waste, agricultural runoff, and urban contaminants pollute salmon-bearing rivers, compromising water quality. These pollutants impair salmon development, reduce reproductive success, and increase vulnerability to disease. As stewards of God's creation, we must not only marvel at the salmon's perseverance but also protect the waters they depend on. Stronger environmental regulations, local clean-up efforts, sustainable farming, and increased public awareness are essential to safeguarding both salmon populations and the larger web of life they support. The story of the salmon reminds us — what we do upstream, both physically and spiritually, matters.

CREATION'S GROANING AND OUR CALL TO HEAL

But despite these remarkable testimonies of life and resilience, creation also tells another story—a groaning one. Though the earth proclaims God's glory, it now bears the wounds of human action—pollution, exploitation, extinction, and neglect. When we harm the earth, we harm the very stage on which God's presence is revealed and upon which human life depends. When soil is degraded, water poisoned, or air polluted, it is the vulnerable, children, the poor, the marginalized, who suffer most. Environmental degradation becomes a form of injustice. To ignore creation care is to neglect

---

5. Brooks, *What's Destroying Pacific Salmon.*

the wellbeing of our neighbors and to fail in our calling as stewards of God's world.

This moment calls us to a deeper, more holistic response, one that unites ecological responsibility with human dignity and spiritual worship. Faithful stewardship involves more than good intentions. It requires spiritual conviction, ethical courage, and informed action. A holistic mindset helps us trace the ripple effects of our decisions, revealing how small acts of care or neglect echo through communities and ecosystems.

When we restore what has been broken, preserve what sustains life, and protect what is vulnerable, we reflect the heart of a Redeemer who is making all things new (Rev 21:5). In doing so, we live as covenant partners, honoring God, serving our neighbors, and nurturing the flourishing of all creation.

THE RESTORATION MANDATE: FROM MICROPLASTICS TO GREEN CHEMISTRY

Have you ever wondered what happens to a plastic bottle after you toss it? What if it ended up inside the brain? These microscopic fragments, shed from synthetic materials, have infiltrated our oceans, soils, and even the human body. Their widespread presence disrupts ecosystems, endangers wildlife, and enters the food chain, standing in stark contrast to God's intention for a flourishing and fruitful creation.

A recent study published in Nature Medicine (2025), titled "Bioaccumulation of Microplastics in Decedent Human Brains[6]," reveals alarming findings: micro, and nanoplastics (MNPs) have been detected in vital human organs, including the liver, kidneys, and brain. Using electron microscopy, researchers identified polyethylene, a common plastic, as the dominant polymer in brain tissue, where it appears as sharp flakes and shards. Between 2016 and 2024, concentrations of these particles in human tissues

---

6. Smith, *Bioaccumulation of Microplastics*, 126.

rose dramatically, with brain tissue showing to 30 times higher accumulation than other organs.

As stewards of God's creation, we are not merely observers of damage but active participants in restoration. Responding faithfully means rethinking our dependence on petroleum-based plastics and embracing sustainable alternatives. This pursuit reflects God's original design, where human creativity serves not exploitation but life-giving, restorative purposes.

Green chemistry[7] provides a framework for designing chemical products and processes that reduce or eliminate hazardous substances. It invites us to create not with exploitation, but with care, safety, and long-term sustainability in mind.

This scientific approach aligns with our call to be restorers. By using renewable feedstocks, biodegradable materials, and non-toxic processes, green chemistry empowers us to reverse harm and honor creation. It helps us reimagine waste not as an inevitable byproduct, but as something preventable, redirected by wisdom and intention.

One powerful response to microplastic pollution is the exploration of bioplastic materials made from renewable resources like starch[8], cellulose[9], or proteins[10]. These materials degrade more easily and pose fewer long-term risks to ecosystems and health. For example:

- Starch-based bioplastics (from corn, potatoes, or tapioca) are used in compostable packaging and utensils.
- Cellulose-based fibers (from wood) are used in films and biodegradable wrappers.
- Protein-based plastics (from dairy or soy) can be used in food packaging, textiles, or even medical tools.

---

7. Anastas and Warner, *Green Chemistry*, 30.
8. Siqueira et al., *Starch-Based Biodegradable Plastics*, 122–130.
9. Das et al., *Cellulose-Based Natural Nanofibers*, 528–544.
10. Bhaskar et al., *Protein-Based Biopolymers*, 108097.

The Earth

Activity: Creating Casein Bioplastic from Milk

This simple experiment invites students to create a biodegradable plastic using milk and acid (like vinegar or lemon juice)[11]. The key ingredient is casein, a milk protein that forms curds when acidified and can be molded into various shapes. Once dried, the curds harden into a plastic-like material.

This activity models several Green Chemistry Principles[12], including:
- Waste prevention
- Use of renewable feedstocks
- Design of safer materials
- Energy efficiency (low-temperature process)

It also introduces basic scientific concepts like protein precipitation, polymer formation, and materials design, through the lens of sustainability.

PROCEDURE: MAKING BIOPLASTIC FROM SOUR MILK

1. **Measure the Milk**
   Use a measuring cylinder to measure 50 mL of sour skimmed milk. Pour it into a 100 mL beaker.

2. **Heat the Milk**
   Place the beaker on a stirrer hot plate and heat the milk to 60 °C. Monitor the temperature with a thermometer and stir gently with a glass rod.

3. **Prepare the Acid**
   While heating, measure 3 mL of lemon juice (or vinegar) using a small measuring cylinder.

4. **Add the Acid**
   Once your milk is hot (around 60 °C), carefully remove it.

---

11. Jefferson et al., *Valorization of Sour Milk*, 1073–1076.
12. American Chemical Society, *12 Principles of Green Chemistry*.

5. **Form the Curds**
   Add the lemon juice to the hot milk and stir gently for about 5 seconds. You'll see white curds begin to form—this is casein!

6. **Separate the Solids**
   Use a spatula to scrape out the curds. Place them on a paper towel and gently press to remove excess water.

7. **Shape the Bioplastic**
   Flatten the damp casein and use a shape cutter to mold it as desired.

8. **Dry the Bioplastic**
   Place your shape on a Petri dish and put it in an oven at 65 °C for 4 hours.

9. **Cool and Share**
   Let your bioplastic cool completely before handling or displaying.

REFLECTION QUESTIONS

1. What does it mean for the Earth to belong to God—and not to us?

2. How does recognizing God's ownership of creation shape the way we view land, wildlife, and resources—such as salmon runs, bald eagle recovery, or ocean pollution?

3. How can studying science become a way to encounter or worship God?

4. What does it mean to participate in restoring God's original design in a broken world?

5. Where in your own context do you see opportunities for faithful stewardship?

2

Rooted and Flourishing
The Story of Trees in Scripture and Nature

THE VITAL LIFE OF TREES

AMONG ALL THE WONDERS God created, trees hold a uniquely significant place. From Genesis to Revelation, they whisper the story of God's presence, provision, and purpose. With roots anchored deep in the earth and branches reaching toward the sky, trees stand as living bridges between soil and heaven, silent sentinels of blessing. In every season, they extend what they receive: bearing fruit, offering shade, and providing shelter, revealing God's faithfulness and sustaining life.

Trees play a vital role in regulating the earth's climate. They absorb carbon dioxide, release water vapor through transpiration, and stabilize ecosystems, preserving the delicate balance of life. Their roots prevent soil erosion, enrich the earth, and support microbial communities that recycle nutrients, sustain plant growth, and maintain healthy ecosystems. Trees also protect themselves with essential oils, repelling pests and attracting helpful allies, which humans have found useful in healing balms, salves, and scents.

Even after their time rooted in the ground is complete, trees continue to give. As wood, they provide beams, boards, and paper, carrying wisdom, stories, and human creativity. Over long timescales, some become peat or coal, fuels that have powered homes and nations.

In the life cycle of a tree, we glimpse the gospel mystery of death and resurrection. A seed must fall and die before it brings life. A tree sheds its leaves, stands bare through winter, then bursts forth anew. Even when cut down, new shoots may rise from the stump. Long after falling, the tree continues to give, its body fuels new life. Creation quietly echoes the greater story: in Christ, death is not the end but the door to restoration, renewal, and resurrection.

Trees are composed of remarkable building blocks, chiefly cellulose and lignin, which give wood strength and flexibility. These materials have modern applications: cellulose forms biodegradable plastics, sustainable textiles, and paper products, while lignin is finding new roles in biofuels, adhesives, and carbon fibers. Such innovations embody the spirit of the UN Sustainable Development Goal 12 (Responsible Consumption and Production), urging us to reduce waste and create responsibly from renewable resources[1].

Forests also shelter biodiversity, enrich soil, and protect watersheds. This echoes UNSDG 15: Life on Land, which calls us to protect and restore ecosystems[2]. Caring for trees and land is ultimately honoring both creation and the Creator who planted them with wisdom. Trees represent character: solid, strong, steadfast, resilient, and true. They have supported civilizations, providing shelter, fuel, tools, and materials for homes and communities. Their roots run deep, anchoring them through storms; their trunks stand tall with quiet strength. Trees sustain life and symbolize the virtues that uphold human progress.

---

1 United Nations, "Goal 12," UN Sustainable Development Goals.
2. United Nations, "Goal 15," UN Sustainable Development Goals.

TREES IN THE BIBLICAL NARRATIVE

The Tree of Life in Genesis: Dependence Designed

The Bible begins and ends with a tree. In Genesis, the tree of life stands at Eden's center, a picture of life fully dependent on God. Humanity was created to live in continual trust, drawing strength from his presence, like trees nourished by deep roots. But when Adam and Eve reached for the tree of the knowledge of good and evil, seeking independence, that relationship was broken. The way to the tree of life was closed, and with it, the fullness of life was lost. Yet God did not abandon his purpose. In Revelation 2:7b, he promises, "To the one who is victorious, I will give the right to eat from the tree of life, which is in the paradise of God." This restoration calls us back to our original design, to live in dependence on God.

The Promise of New Life: The Shoot from Jesse's Stump

Though dependence was broken, redemption continued. Isaiah prophesied, "A shoot will come up from the stump of Jesse" (Isa 11:1). From what seemed lifeless, God would bring new life, fulfilled in Christ, the true and living branch. Rooted deeply in human flesh yet fully connected to the Father, Jesus embodies both humanity and divinity. His coming is God visiting us as man, taking on our nature, sharing our experience, and restoring our broken dependence. As Isaiah describes, "For he grew up like a tender plant before him, and like a root out of dry ground. He has no attracting form nor majesty that we should look upon him, nor beautiful appearance that we should desire him" (Isa 53:2). In this humble, unassuming form, Jesus, whom we know as the Son of Man, reveals the profound mystery of God's presence with us in human form.

The Tree of the Cross: The Turning Point of History

In 1 Peter, we learn Christ bore our sins on the "tree" (1 Pet 2:24). The cross, once a symbol of death and curse, becomes the turning point where death is undone and life is reopened. This tree reverses the curse, restoring hope and reconciliation.

The Healing Tree at Marah: A Shadow of the Cross

Long before the cross, God showed healing through a tree (Exod 15:25). When the Israelites cried out, God told Moses to cast a tree into bitter waters, making them sweet. This points forward to Christ, lifted on the cross, who brings life and healing to all who believe.

The Vine and the Branches: Union Restored

Being truly connected to life is like a branch to a vine. Humanity was placed near the tree of life but cut off by sin (Gen 3:24). Yet Jesus declares, "I am the vine; you are the branches" (John 15:5), revealing that through him we are united with the source of life. What was outside our reach becomes our inner reality. Growth and transformation flow from this hidden spiritual connection (1 Cor 6:17, Rom 8:16). Like a branch drawing life from the vine, we flourish when joined to Christ, not by striving but by abiding. Thus, the Christian life is built not by outward effort, but by inward fellowship, life flowing from God.

The Olive Tree: Grafted into God's Family

Paul describes Gentiles as wild branches grafted into a cultivated olive tree (Rom 11:17). By grace, we share in God's root system, no longer outsiders but partakers of his life, drawing strength, purpose, and identity from his promises.

The Tree of Life in Revelation: Dependence Fully Restored

Genesis shows humanity cut off from the tree of life; the Gospels reveal Christ as the true Vine; the Epistles show us grafted in. This abiding union, once lost, is now present reality. In Revelation, the tree of life stands again, yielding fruit each month and leaves for healing, fed by the river flowing from God's throne (Rev 22:2). What began with separation ends in restored dependence, perfect, eternal, and overflowing with life.

Planted in His Presence: Trees as Flourishing Humanity

Between Genesis and Revelation, trees appear at pivotal moments of divine encounter. At the burning bush, a tree burned without being consumed, and Moses met God (Exod 3). By a tamarisk tree in Beersheba, Abraham called on the eternal God (Gen 21:33), planting testimony that the hidden, everlasting One was his refuge.

Palm trees symbolize flourishing life under God's care (Ps 92:12), rejoicing in victory (Lev 23:40; Neh 8:15; John 12:13; Rev 7:9). Ps 92:12–15 celebrates them flourishing in the courts of God, still bearing fruit in old age, full of sap and green, radiating vitality, resilience, and strength.

Trees were integral to worship and God's dwelling. The Tabernacle's boards were made from acacia wood overlaid with gold (Exod 26:26—29). The Temple used cypress, cedar, and olive. The miraculous budding of Aaron's rod (Num 17:8) affirmed God's authority and pointed to resurrection and renewal—the lifeless placed in God's presence bringing new life.

A LIVING PARABLE: THE TRINITY REVEALED IN EVERY LEAF

As we explore the science of trees, we find a deeper spiritual truth reflected in their life-giving processes. The process of photosynthesis reveals a divine metaphor. A tree takes in carbon dioxide, water, and light, transforming them into glucose and oxygen. This process sustains life. Spiritually, it reflects the Triune God—Father, Son, and Holy Spirit—working in perfect unity to give life.

Carbon is foundational to all organic life. Though it enters the tree as carbon dioxide from the atmosphere (CO_2), what the tree does with it is astonishing. This life element becomes the backbone of glucose, the energy source that fuels growth. Its unparalleled ability to bond with itself and other elements allows it to form life's most essential molecules: DNA, carbohydrates, proteins, and lipids.

The carbon in carbon dioxide symbolizes Christ, who came to give life, and life abundantly (John 10:10). Just as carbon forms the backbone of all life's molecules, Christ is the unseen yet essential foundation of spiritual life and growth. In him, "all things hold together" (Col 1:17). If anyone is in Christ, he is a new creation; the old things have passed away, behold, new things have come (2 Cor 5:17). And he who is joined to the LORD is one spirit with him, the humble yet unshakable binding force of creation and new creation alike (1 Cor 6:17).

Water, drawn from roots, is essential for photosynthesis, transporting nutrients and enabling the production of glucose that sustains a tree's life. In Scripture, water often symbolizes life in the Spirit. Jesus offers the Samaritan woman "living water" at the well (John 4), representing the eternal life and spiritual sustenance he provides, promising that those who drink will never thirst again. Likewise, in John 7:37–38, he declares, "If anyone thirsts, let him come to me and drink. Whoever believes in me . . . rivers of living water will flow from within them." This living water represents the Spirit, the divine presence that refreshes, nourishes, and transforms believers from within. Just as water flows upward through roots to sustain the tree, so the Spirit flows through believers, nurturing spiritual growth and enabling the fruit of the Spirit to flourish.

Light powers photosynthesis, providing the energy trees need to transform water and carbon dioxide into life-sustaining glucose. In a profound spiritual parallel, Scripture declares, "God is light, and in him is no darkness at all" (1 John 1:5). The old creation came into being through God's spoken word, as described in Genesis, where he said, "Let there be light." In the new creation, God brings life and transformation through his shining. Paul writes in 2 Corinthians 4:6, "For God, who said, 'Let light shine out of darkness,' has shone in our hearts to give the light of the knowledge of the glory of God in the face of Jesus Christ." Just as God's voice brought forth physical light that sustained the world, his shining now illuminates our hearts, revealing Christ's glory and imparting spiritual life. This profound connection highlights how divine light sustains both creation and new creation, guiding believers from darkness into the radiance of God's presence.

Finally, just as photosynthesis releases oxygen vital for sustaining physical life, Christ indwells believers, breathing spiritual life into their inner being. The oxygen quietly given by trees sustains our bodies, just as Christ's presence continually sustains our spirit (John 20:22; 1 Cor 15:45b). He is the breath of life within us, renewing and empowering us moment by moment. All we need to do is call on him, for as Acts 2:21 declares, "And it shall be that everyone who calls on the name of the LORD shall be saved."

THE HIDDEN LIFE: ROOTED IN THE UNSEEN

What we see, the leaves and branches, is only part of the story. True strength lies in the roots beneath the soil. They anchor the tree, draw water and nutrients, and store reserves. Without this hidden foundation, no leaf would unfurl or fruit form. Likewise, our spiritual strength grows in hiddenness, prayer, surrender, faithfulness when no one watches (Matt 6:6). Our roots, grown in quietness, determine our ability to stand firm and bear fruit.

The psalmist writes, "He is like a tree planted by streams of water . . . " whose leaf does not wither" (Ps 1:3). Jeremiah says it "does not fear when heat comes . . . never fails to bear fruit" (Jer 17:8). Hosea paints a picture of stability and flourishing (Hosea 14:5-6). Paul exhorts, "Continue to live your lives in him, rooted and built up in him, strengthened in faith" (Col 2:6–7). Christ is the rich soil that sustains us.

Jesus often withdrew into quiet places to meet with God in secret (Luke 5:16; Matt 14:23), even sending away the crowds to spend time alone with the Father. This practice reflects a pattern seen with the Israelites, who gathered manna each morning, daily receiving God's provision. Establishing a daily morning practice of spending intentional time with the LORD is foundational to growing in faith and spiritual maturity. This quiet fellowship with God sets the tone for the day, grounding us in his presence and guidance. By embracing practical habits and principles, we can nurture and strengthen this sacred routine, allowing our relationship with God to deepen continually. The life that endures is planted deep, quiet, hidden, and real. The unseen roots allow branches to rise higher and truer.

THE HIDDEN NETWORK OF COMMUNION: A PICTURE OF THE BODY OF CHRIST

No tree grows alone. Beneath the soil, roots connect through fungi called mycelium. This partnership, known as mycorrhiza, is not merely a transaction exchanging sugars for water and minerals; it is a true communion. These fungal networks link tree to tree, species to species, forming a vast "Wood Wide Web." Older trees nourish younger ones, and the strong support the weak. Warnings and nutrients flow through this network of grace, echoing Scripture: "If one part suffers, every part suffers with it; if one part is honored, every part rejoices with it" (1 Cor 12:26).

This serves as a powerful image for the Body of Christ. We are not isolated individuals but deeply connected. "We, though many, are one body in Christ" (Rom 12:5). Rooted in Christ and joined together in love, we share in his life. He humbled himself to lift the weak, forming a Body where every member matters.

FAITHFUL STEWARDS OF TREES AND BEYOND

Trees are life itself—pillars of ecological health and human well-being. Their benefits extend far beyond the forest, reaching into medicine and healing. Over nearly four decades, more than 32 percent of approved small-molecule drugs have come directly from natural sources, many derived from trees. In cancer treatment, nearly 65 percent of new small-molecule therapies were either natural or inspired by nature.[3] This remarkable medicinal potential reveals the profound wisdom woven into creation by God.

At the same time, human use of chemistry in agriculture presents significant challenges. Pesticides help protect food security, but they also carry risks including neurotoxicity, hormonal disruption, and links to cancer. These chemicals often persist in soil and water, harming ecosystems and ultimately returning to us through the food we eat and the water we drink. Although hazardous pesticides like DDT have been banned in many countries, many harmful substances remain in use around the world.

This tension exposes a fundamental contradiction between human convenience and our biblical mandate to care for the Earth. As faithful stewards, we are called to exercise wisdom, restraint, and responsibility in how we apply scientific knowledge. Our goal must be to ensure that science serves life rather than causing harm.

From the soil beneath our feet to the heights of the heavens, trees stand as living witnesses to God's faithful presence and abundant provision. They remind us to be deeply rooted in him, to grow together in loving community, and to embrace our calling as caretakers of creation with care, hope, and joy. Stewardship calls us to protect and preserve the natural world as a sacred trust given by God. Just as the tree of life symbolizes eternal sustenance, Christ is our root, refuge, and source of restoration. In him, we are firmly planted to flourish now and forever.

---

3. Newman and Cragg, "Natural Products as Sources of New Drugs," 775

ACTIVITY: MAKING A NATURAL MOSQUITO REPELLENT

In this hands-on activity, students explore the protective power of plants by creating a natural mosquito repellent using essential oils like citronella, geranium, thyme and eucalyptus. This is more than chemistry—it's an invitation to care. Students are encouraged to take their repellent home as a gift of care for their families.

Option 1: Oil-Based Roll-On

(For direct skin application—not suitable as a spray)

Materials:

- 10 drops each of Citronella, Geranium, Thyme, and Eucalyptus essential oils
- 30 mL fractionated (liquid) coconut oil
- 1 dark glass roll-on bottle (30–50 mL)

Instructions:

1. Add essential oils to the roll-on bottle.
2. Fill the rest of the bottle with coconut oil.
3. Shake well to mix.
4. Apply to pulse points: wrists, ankles, neck.

Option 2: Water-Based Spray

(Recommended for clothing, air, and light skin use)

Materials:

- 10 drops each of Citronella, Geranium, Thyme, and Eucalyptus essential oils
- 15 mL witch hazel (as emulsifier)
- 120 mL distilled water
- Optional: 1 tsp vegetable glycerin (for added moisture)
- Clean 4 oz spray bottle

Instructions:

1. Add essential oils and witch hazel to the spray bottle.
2. Shake well to emulsify.
3. Add distilled water. Shake again.
4. Label clearly. Store in a cool, dark place.
5. Shake before each use. Spray on clothing or exposed skin (avoid face/eyes).

Green Chemistry Connection:

This activity aligns with these Green Chemistry Principles[4]:
- Designing safer chemicals
- Safer solvents and auxiliaries
- Use of renewable feedstocks
- Design for degradation

---

4. American Chemical Society, "12 Principles of Green Chemistry."

REFLECTION QUESTIONS

1. What does it mean to be "rooted" in God, like a tree drawing life from its source? How might this image change the way you think about your spiritual life?

2. Trees grow together as a community, connected beneath the surface. How does this shape your view of your role in your local church or community?

3. How do the biblical stories of trees—from Eden to Revelation—reveal God's presence and purpose in your life? Where do you see evidence of new life and restoration in your own story?

4. In what ways are you called to steward the natural world around you? What practical steps can you take to care for creation with hope and joy?

5. Reflect on the idea that photosynthesis is a living parable of the Trinity at work. How does this enrich your understanding of God's sustaining power in your daily life.

3

Living Water
The Flow of God's Life

THE SCIENCE OF WATER: GOD'S DESIGN FOR LIFE

WATER IS ONE OF the most extraordinary substances known to science, essential for all life and fundamental to the physical universe[1]. Its molecular structure is deceptively simple, composed of two hydrogen atoms bonded to one oxygen atom, yet its polarity gives it properties that are nothing short of life-sustaining. Because water molecules are polar, they are drawn to each other by hydrogen bonds. Each individual hydrogen bond is weak, but together they create a powerful network that grants water remarkable abilities without which life could not exist.

One of these abilities is cohesion, the tendency of water molecules to cling to each other, which results in surface tension. This invisible film allows certain insects to walk across ponds and enables droplets to bead on leaves. Water also adheres to other surfaces, a property that enables capillary action. This subtle but

---

1. Spellman, *The Science of Water*, 2018.

vital process draws water upward through the narrow vessels of plants, delivering dissolved nutrients from roots to leaves.

Another remarkable feature is water's high specific heat capacity, which allows it to absorb large amounts of heat with minimal change in temperature. This stabilizes climates, protects organisms from rapid temperature shifts, and buffers the environments in which life thrives. Water also has a high heat of vaporization, enabling it to remove excess heat through evaporation, a cooling process that helps regulate body temperature in animals through mechanisms such as sweating.

Even in its solid form, water behaves unlike most substances. Rather than contracting as it freezes, it expands, becoming less dense than its liquid form. Ice floats, forming an insulating layer that shields aquatic life during winter months. Without this anomaly, entire ecosystems would perish in frozen bodies of water.

Because of its polarity, water acts as a universal solvent, capable of dissolving more substances than any other liquid. This is critical for life's chemistry, as it allows nutrients, gases such as oxygen and carbon dioxide, and metabolic wastes to dissolve and move freely within organisms. Ionic compounds such as sodium chloride separate into their constituent ions when surrounded by water molecules, preventing recombination and enabling biological transport. Polar organic molecules such as sugars and amino acids dissolve through hydrogen bonding or dipole interactions, ensuring that biochemical reactions proceed efficiently.

Within living organisms, water's roles are as diverse as they are indispensable. Cells, which are composed of 70 to 90 percent water, rely on it to provide the medium in which molecular interactions occur, to maintain shape, and to preserve the selective permeability of membranes. Water regulates body temperature, cushions organs, maintains blood volume, and supports homeostasis. It forms the bulk of blood and lymph in animals, carrying oxygen, nutrients, and wastes to and from cells. In plants, it transports dissolved minerals upward from roots, fueling photosynthesis and growth.

Beyond its role within organisms, water shapes Earth's systems on a grand scale. It naturally exists as a solid, liquid, and gas, cycling between these states to regulate climate and weather. Its evaporation and condensation redistribute heat across the planet, driving atmospheric patterns. Its surface tension and capillary action sustain plant life, while its heat capacity stabilizes ecosystems against fluctuations that could otherwise threaten life. From the cellular level to the planetary scale, water's properties reflect a balance and order that enable life to flourish. Its chemical simplicity masks an intricacy of design that points to both the precision of natural laws and the providence of the Creator who set them in place.

WATER AT THE EDGE OF LAND: WHERE RESILIENCE THRIVES

Where water meets land, these properties reveal their full power. Along coastlines, rivers, and estuaries, water sculpts the earth with patient persistence. Over time, it carves valleys, shapes cliffs, and smooths rocky shores. Waves erode coastlines while rivers carry sediments to form fertile deltas and estuaries, creating rich habitats for countless species. In these borderlands between water and soil, life thrives in remarkable abundance.

One of the most striking examples is found in mangrove forests. These trees grow in the shifting, saline soils of tropical and subtropical coasts, where few plants can survive. Their tangled roots anchor them against waves and tides, filter salt from seawater, and provide shelter from storms. Beneath the surface, these roots form nurseries for fish, crustaceans, and other marine life, sustaining entire food webs that stretch far beyond the mangroves themselves. Such ecosystems demonstrate not only water's ability to sustain life but also nature's capacity to adapt and flourish under challenging conditions.

Saltwater environments such as coral reefs, estuaries, and seagrass beds are among the most productive ecosystems on earth. Despite the constant forces of tides, waves, and salinity, they teem with life from microscopic plankton to large marine mammals. Water's capacity to circulate nutrients, mix salinity, and regulate temperature creates dynamic conditions in which biodiversity thrives.

This interplay of water and land also teaches lessons about resilience and renewal. In the meeting of salt and soil, erosion and growth, there is a balance sustained by constant movement. Shorelines change, habitats shift, and yet life adapts, replenishes, and endures. Such patterns mirror the Creator's wisdom in designing a world where transformation is woven into the very fabric of existence. Yet every wave, tide, and droplet that meets the shore begins its journey far away, in the silent heights where mountains and rocks cradle the world's most enduring sources of fresh water.

WATER'S JOURNEY FROM ROCK AND MOUNTAIN: NATURE'S WATER TOWERS

Mountains and rocks are among the most important sources of the world's freshwater. Acting as natural reservoirs, they capture snow, ice, and rain, storing it in glaciers, lakes, and underground aquifers. Over time, this stored water is gradually released through springs, streams, and rivers, supplying life far beyond the mountain slopes. Scientists often refer to mountains as the "water towers" of the world because they provide freshwater to over half of humanity. The Himalayas, for example, feed some of Asia's greatest rivers such as the Ganges, Yangtze, and Mekong, sustaining billions of people.

Rock formations play a vital role in this process. Water seeps into cracks and pores in the rock, where it is filtered and stored before emerging as springs. Limestone and sandstone, in particular, are known for their ability to hold and release water. This natural filtration not only makes the water cleaner but also helps regulate its flow, ensuring a steady supply even during dry seasons.

As these streams descend from high places, they sometimes take dramatic leaps over cliffs, forming waterfalls that display both beauty and power. Mist rises like a veil, rainbows appear in the spray, and the sound of rushing water fills the air with life. These falls are more than scenic wonders; they oxygenate the water, nourish surrounding plants, and sustain thriving ecosystems below.

From the snowy cascades of the Alps to the thunderous drops of the Andes, waterfalls stand as living symbols of abundance and renewal. Just as every river draws its strength from a hidden spring, so all the life-giving waters of the earth point to a greater Source still unseen, waiting to be revealed.

This greater Source is none other than God himself, whose Spirit has been flowing since the beginning of creation.

GOD KEEPS ON FLOWING

In the beginning, the Spirit of God hovered over the face of the waters. From that still and infinite deep, God spoke life into being. Light broke forth, land emerged, oceans formed, and rivers nourished the earth. Waters teemed with creatures, and finally, man was created to dwell in this living world (Gen 1–2).

From Eden's rivers to the wilderness of Sinai, God's presence and provision flowed alongside his people. In the days of Moses, he led Israel out of Egypt through the parted waters of the Red Sea (Exod 14:16), an act the Apostle Paul later called a baptism into Moses (1 Cor 10:1–2). In the barren desert, after feeding them with manna, God satisfied their thirst:

> "I will stand there before you by the rock at Horeb. Strike the rock, and water will come out of it for the people to drink." — Exodus 17:6

Moses struck the rock, and water poured forth. This miracle met their physical need and pointed to something greater. Paul reveals the mystery: "They drank from the spiritual rock that followed them, and the rock was Christ" (1 Cor 10:4). Christ, the true Rock, was struck once on the cross, and from his side flowed blood and water (John 19:34), signifying both redemption and life.

Later, when the people again thirsted, God gave a new instruction:

> "Speak to that rock before their eyes and it will pour out its water." — Numbers 20:8

This change was profound. The Rock did not need to be struck again. Christ's sacrifice was once for all. Now the living water flows when we simply come in faith and speak.

When Jesus spoke with Nicodemus, he revealed the deeper meaning of this living water. "Unless one is born of water and the Spirit, he cannot enter the kingdom of God" (John 3:5). Baptism became the sign of this new birth. As Paul writes, "Or don't you know that all of us who were baptized into Christ Jesus were baptized into his death? We were therefore buried with him through baptism into death in order that, just as Christ was raised from the dead through the glory of the Father, we too may live a new life" (Rom 6:3–4).

At Jacob's well in Samaria, Jesus met a woman carrying not only her water jar but also the weight of her past. Their conversation turned from physical thirst to a deeper longing:

> "If you knew the gift of God and who it is that asks you for a drink, you would have asked him and he would have given you living water" (John 4:10).

> "but whoever drinks the water I give them will never thirst. Indeed, the water I give them will become in them a spring of water welling up to eternal life." — John 4:14

Here, Jesus is not only the giver of water. He is the Living Water. To receive him is to be inwardly renewed and satisfied at the deepest level of the soul. The Samaritan woman drank and her life was transformed. Her jar was left behind. Her thirst was gone.

This living water is God's life in Christ, the very center of salvation and the goal of human redemption. Christ gave himself on the cross to release this water of life. He rose again and became the life-giving Spirit, able to enter into all who believe (John 7:39; 1 Cor 15:45).

Living Water

When the Spirit enters, we do not merely receive help; we receive Christ himself as living water, the only One who can truly satisfy the human soul. His life quenches our inner thirst and becomes in us a fountain springing up into eternal life. The woman at the well was satisfied when she received the Living Water—and so was Jesus.

> "Out of his innermost being shall flow rivers of living water." — John 7:38

The water Jesus gives is not meant to remain static. It moves. It springs up. It flows out. This is the nature of true spiritual life—it overflows.

From a well in Samaria to a fountain in our hearts, the story of living water flows through all of Scripture and finds its glorious consummation in Revelation:

> "Then the angel showed me the river of the water of life, as clear as crystal, flowing from the throne of God and of the Lamb down the middle of the great street of the city." — Revelation 22:1-2

This is the water Jesus promised, the water he released at the cross, the water that becomes in us a fountain springing up to eternal life. In the new creation, this river flows freely and abundantly—not from human effort or religious striving, but from the throne of the Lamb, who gave himself so we might drink.

This is our destiny: nourished forever by the water of life, our thirst eternally quenched, our joy made full. And even now, we begin to taste that joy, as Isaiah foretold:

> "With joy you will draw water from the wells of salvation."
> — Isaiah 12:3

Yet this living water is not only a gift to be received; it calls for a response. God invites each of us to come with open hearts and drink deeply by faith. As the Spirit and the Bride declare in Revelation, "Let the one who is thirsty come; and let the one who desires take the water of life without price" (Rev 22:17). This invitation is personal and urgent — a call to step forward and receive the fullness of life that only Christ can give. When we respond in faith, we enter into a living relationship where his Spirit becomes an ever-flowing fountain within us, refreshing our souls and overflowing into every area of our lives.

From creation to eternity, God has been flowing, supplying, refreshing, and restoring. The Rock has been struck once. The water is free. The invitation still stands.

WATER POLLUTION AND OUR RESPONSIBILITY

Despite water's vital role in sustaining life, it is increasingly threatened by pollution from human activities. Dye effluents from textile industries, for example, release toxic and persistent chemicals into waterways, harming aquatic ecosystems and contaminating drinking water. This pollution not only disrupts natural cycles but also affects communities reliant on clean water. As stewards of God's creation, we are called to care for water responsibly, understanding the chemistry behind pollutants and applying sustainable practices to minimize harm. This chapter's tie-dyeing activity revisits a common, colorful experiment with a green chemistry lens. It teaches how to remove dye from wastewater before disposal and demonstrates practical ways to protect our precious water resources.

ACTIVITY: TIE-DYEING A T-SHIRT[2]

Tie-dyeing is a familiar childhood activity, yet it can also serve as a bioinspired and safer alternative to a standard introductory organic chemistry experiment. Using water-soluble Procion reactive dyes, students dye cellulose cotton fibers in a process designed for biodegradability and reusability. The reaction produces no waste and yields a tie-dyed T-shirt that can be worn, reused, and ultimately biodegraded, connecting classroom

---

2. Abraham, *Green Nucleophilic Aromatic Substitution*, 3810.

chemistry to real-world applications. Through this hands-on experience, students develop essential laboratory skills, explore the link between chemistry and the environment, and recognize how chemical choices affect both human and ecological wellbeing. Since about 20 percent of dye molecules remain unfixed to the fabric and would typically be washed into common sewage, the activity challenges students to remove this excess dye before disposal, fostering a mindset of environmental stewardship.

Procedure (For Two Students)

Safety First: Wear a dust mask when handling powdered dyes and sodium carbonate.

PART I: Dyeing the T-Shirts

- Dissolve 45.0 g sodium carbonate (Na_2CO_3) in 750 mL warm water.
- Soak the cotton T-shirts in this solution for 20–30 minutes.
- After soaking, gently squeeze out the excess liquid (do not rinse).
- Use three dyes: Fuchsia Red, Lemon Yellow, and Turquoise. For each color: Weigh 2.7 g of dye powder into a 250 mL beaker. Add a small amount of hot water to dissolve the dye. Then add more water to make 75.0 mL total solution. Pour each dye solution into its own squeeze bottle.
- Fold and tie the pre-soaked T-shirts using rubber bands or string.
- Apply the dyes with squeeze bottles—use as many colors as you wish!
- Be sure to saturate both the front and back thoroughly.

- Once dyed, place the T-shirts into sealed plastic bags. Allow them to cure for at least 4 hours (preferably 24 hours for best color intensity).
- With the ties still on, rinse each T-shirt under cold running water.
- Then switch to warm water, untying the T-shirt as you rinse. Continue rinsing until the water runs fairly clear. Important: Collect all rinse water in a container for use in Part II.

PART II: Wastewater Purification

- Remove Dye from Wastewater Using Activated Charcoal
- Add activated charcoal to the collected rinse water.
- Stir thoroughly to allow the dye molecules to adsorb onto the charcoal. Let it sit briefly, then filter the solution if needed. Once the water appears clear and colorless, it is safe to pour down the sink.

REFLECTION QUESTIONS

- Reflect on John 4 and John 7. What does it mean to have a spring of living water within you?
- In what ways does the biblical imagery of living water speak to your personal spiritual thirst and renewal?
- How do you personally experience the living water Jesus offers in your daily life?
- What does it mean that living water flows not only inwardly but also outwardly, impacting those around you?
- Why is caring for and protecting water resources an important expression of your faith and stewardship of God's creation?

4

Precious Stones
God's Transformation Work to Form His House

FROM DUST TO GLORY: THE DIVINE PURPOSE IN PRECIOUS STONES

THE BIBLE OPENS WITH a garden filled not only with plants and animals but also with precious minerals and stones. Genesis mentions rivers flowing through Eden, rich with gold, bdellium, and onyx. "The gold of that land is good; bdellium and onyx stone are there" (Gen 2:12). Even in the beginning, precious stones point beyond themselves to God's purpose of transforming earthly materials into his eternal dwelling.

Throughout Scripture, precious stones symbolize God's transformative work. They symbolize beauty, refinement, strength, and identity. God is not just saving individuals, he is building a house, a spiritual house culminating in the New Jerusalem. We, the redeemed and transformed, are the living materials God uses to build his eternal house.

The Breastplate of Twelve Stones: God's Covenant People

The high priest of Israel wore a breastplate of twelve precious stones, each bearing the name of a tribe (Exo 28). These stones symbolized the people, formed from dust and called into God's presence. The breastplate was a prototype of the spiritual house God is building, a unified community shaped by covenant, trial, and destined for glory. It reminds us that God carries his people before him, continually guiding and shaping them.

God the Rock: The Unshakable Foundation

No house can stand without a firm foundation. God is often described as a Rock, steadfast, faithful, and unmovable (Ps 18:2). The Israelites drank water from a rock in the wilderness, a sign of God's presence and provision. Paul reveals this rock as a picture of Christ, who sustains and transforms us despite our failings (1 Cor 10:4).

When Moses was placed in the cleft of the rock to see God's glory (Exod 33:22), it foreshadowed Christ, the Rock who was wounded and cleft for us. Jesus declared to Peter, "Upon this rock I will build my church" (Matt 16:18), establishing himself as the unshakable foundation of God's house.

God is quietly shaping and preparing us in the quarry of daily life, carving and polishing so that when assembled, his house rises in glory without noise or strife (1 Kings 6:7).

From Clay to Stone: Spirit-led Refinement

We begin as clay, malleable and fragile (Isa 64:8). But clay alone cannot endure. It must be refined by fire, tested and purified (Isa 48:10; Zech 13:9). This refining is the work of the Spirit, who shapes us and fills us with life.

Paul describes this transformation as beholding the glory of the LORD and being changed into his image by the Spirit (2 Cor 3:18). We are renewed and strengthened by the Spirit flowing within us (Eph 3:16-17). We are not hollow shells but living stones, saturated with God's presence.

Christ: Cornerstone and Living Stone

At the heart of God's building project is Christ, the foundation stone on which everything rests (1 Cor 3:11) and the cornerstone shaping the entire structure (Eph 2:20; Ps 118:22). In him, the whole building grows into a holy temple (Eph 2:21), and we are being built together into a dwelling place for God's Spirit (Eph 2:22).

Though rejected by many, Christ is the living Stone, chosen by God and precious. As we come to him, like newborn babies longing for milk, we grow in our salvation. In coming to this living Stone, we too become living stones, being built into a spiritual house and set apart as a holy priesthood, offering spiritual sacrifices acceptable to God through Jesus Christ (1 Pet 2:2-6). In him, we find our place and purpose within God's eternal house.

He is also the capstone that completes the temple (Zech 4:7; Ep 2:21), and the treasure hidden within our fragile "earthen vessels" (2 Cor 4:7). His life and glory dwell in us as God shapes us into his dwelling place.

Diamonds: Formed by Pressure and Patience

Diamonds remind us of the power and patience of God's transformation. Deep in the Earth's mantle, carbon atoms endure immense pressure and heat, slowly becoming brilliant stones prized for their strength and beauty.

This process, requiring both intense pressure and high temperature over millions of years, mirrors our spiritual growth. Like diamonds, we are transformed from ordinary material into something precious, enduring, and radiant.

Paul teaches that God himself sanctifies us completely—spirit, soul, and body—preserving us until Christ returns (1 Thess

5:23–24). This transformation is gradual as our minds are renewed to reflect God's will (Rom 12:2; Eph 4:23).

We endure pressures and trials as diamonds do heat and pressure, yet the life of Jesus is revealed in us (2 Cor 4:7–18). Our present sufferings are light compared to the eternal glory they produce. Though groaning inwardly, we eagerly await full redemption (Rom 8:23).

Metamorphic Rocks: Faith Pressed into Glory

Like metamorphic rocks[1], which form through heat and pressure altering existing stone, our lives are refined by God's Spirit. Though fragile "earthen vessels," we carry his power and glory within (2 Cor 4:7).

We are pressed but not crushed, perplexed but not despairing, struck down but not destroyed (2 Cor 4:8–9). Our outer selves may waste away, but our inner selves are renewed daily (2 Cor 4:16). Our present troubles, though light and momentary, are producing for us an eternal glory that far outweighs them all (2 Cor 4:17). This transformation reminds us to fix our eyes not on what is seen and temporary but on what is unseen and eternal (2 Cor 4:18). Just as metamorphic rocks are shaped and strengthened by intense pressure and heat over time, our faith and character are refined through life's trials, revealing the glory of God within us.

The Geode: Hidden Treasure Revealed

A geode looks ordinary outside but holds a hidden cavity lined with sparkling crystals. Similarly, our outward lives may seem plain, but inside, the Spirit deposits Christ's riches, transforming us into vessels of glory (2 Cor 3:16–18).

Just as mineral-rich water seeps through rock and deposits layers that slowly transform an empty cavity into something

---

1. Garlick, *National Geographic Pocket Guide to Rocks and Minerals of North America*, 2014.

radiant with crystals, so the Spirit flows within us, depositing Christ's riches into our being. When our heart turns to the LORD, the veil is removed (2 Cor. 3:16), and where the Spirit of the LORD is, there is freedom (2 Cor. 3:17). With unveiled faces, as we behold and reflect the glory of the LORD, we are transformed into his image from glory to glory by the LORD Spirit (2 Cor. 3:18). Thus, we are the "earthen vessels" (2 Cor 4:7), plain and fragile yet carrying the treasure of Christ within. Like geodes, our true beauty is hidden within and is revealed only when the outer man is broken.

Petrified Wood: Transformation Through Time

Petrified wood forms when buried wood is slowly replaced by minerals from flowing water. This transformation requires burial, steady flow, and time.

Spiritually, this process resembles our growth—allowing God to permeate us through life's circumstances, bringing resurrection power, peace, and joy even amid challenges (Phil 3:10; 4:4-7; Eph 3:16-17). Inward prayer becomes our response, bringing every concern to God with thanksgiving (Philippians 4:6). Instead of being anxious, we choose to rejoice, trusting that through this journey Christ will be magnified (Phil 4:4; 1:20). As we surrender, his peace rises within us, guarding our hearts and minds even amid challenges (Phil 4:7). The Father, according to the riches of his glory, strengthens us with power through his Spirit into our inner being so that Christ may make his home in our hearts through faith, rooting and grounding us in love (Eph 3:16-17). All our particular situations will turn out for our salvation as we abide in the bountiful supply of the Spirit of Jesus Christ (Phil 1:19).

Obsidian: Beauty Born from Fire

Obsidian forms when molten lava cools rapidly, producing smooth, sharp volcanic glass. Its beauty is born from sudden heat and change.

In faith, sudden trials can produce a tested, enduring hope, much like gold refined by fire (1 Peter 1:6–9). God shapes us in moments of hardship, creating faith that shines with praise and glory.

The New Jerusalem: God's Eternal Dwelling

God's grand building project reaches its fulfillment in the New Jerusalem, described in Revelation 21 as a city radiant with precious stones, streets of pure gold, and gates of pearl, each detail symbolizing the transformation of suffering into eternal glory. John was "carried away in the Spirit onto a great and high mountain" to see this holy city coming down out of heaven from God (Rev 21:10).

The city's brilliance, described as "having the glory of God" and shining like "a most precious stone, like a jasper stone, as clear as crystal" (Rev 21:11), speaks to the overwhelming presence and holiness of God rather than material construction. Its walls, gates, and foundations are symbolic: the twelve gates named after the tribes of Israel, the twelve foundations named for the apostles of the Lamb (Rev 21:12–14), and the streets of pure gold like transparent glass (Rev 21:21) all represent the redeemed people of God, formed and transformed by his grace.

The absence of a temple (Rev 21:22) because "the LORD God Almighty and the Lamb are its temple" emphasizes that God's presence fills and defines the city. The city "has no need of the sun or the moon" because God's glory and the Lamb are its light (Rev 21:23). This transcends any earthly, physical city, indicating an eternal spiritual reality where God and his people dwell in unbroken fellowship.

In the Old Testament, God's dwelling was among his people in the tabernacle and later the temple. In the New Testament, his dwelling is within his people, who are being built together in Christ, the true and living tabernacle and the unshakable foundation of God's house (Matt 16:18). The presence of God within believers—Christ indwelling us (2 Tim 4:22), Christ making his home in our hearts (Eph 3:17), and the Spirit bringing life to our spirit, soul, and body (Rom 8:6, 10-11)—reveals how God works inwardly.

Jesus promises, "On that day you will realize that I am in my Father, and you are in me, and I am in you" (John 14:20), revealing the profound unity between God, Christ, and believers. This intimate indwelling is the very essence of the New Jerusalem, a spiritual city made of living, transformed people joined in eternal fellowship with God.

In this eternal dwelling, the Spirit and the bride invite all who hear to enter: "Come!" Let the one who is thirsty come; and let the one who wishes take the free gift of the water of life (Rev 22:17). This invitation extends the promise of abundant life and unbroken communion with God, flowing from the throne of the Lamb and sustaining his redeemed people forever.

The Singing Stones: Eternal Praise

In Montana and Pennsylvania, there are geological formations where certain stones—often made of resonant minerals like quartzite—can "ring" when struck, much like a bell. These "ringing rocks" are a natural wonder, producing clear tones because of their density, internal stress, and mineral composition. They stand as a vivid picture of creation's readiness to praise, echoing Jesus' words in Luke 19:40 that if people kept silent, even the stones would cry out.

When the New Jerusalem descends, it marks not only the completion of God's building work but also the dawn of unending praise (2 Chron 5:12-13):

"He is good; his love endures forever."

In Revelation, this glory finds its eternal fulfillment—there is no temple in the New Jerusalem, for God himself and the Lamb are its temple (Rev 21:22). The city needs no sun or moon, for the glory of God illuminates it, and the Lamb is its lamp (Rev 21:23). God's presence fills the city completely, and his radiant glory shines forevermore (Rev 22:5).

GOD'S LABORATORY: THE CHEMISTRY OF TRANSFORMATION

Step into a chemistry lab for a moment. You'll find beakers bubbling, crystals forming, solvents swirling through chromatography columns, and distillates dripping into flasks. Behind every reaction is a clear goal: purity, transformation, and purpose.

Much like our spiritual journey, the lab is where ordinary substances undergo extraordinary change. Take chromatography, a mixture is passed through a medium that separates its components. Doesn't the Spirit sometimes do just that, drawing out what doesn't belong?

Distillation? It applies heat to purify, just as trials refine us. Crystallization? Molecules slowly align to form beauty and order. Filtration? It lets the refined pass through, removing the rest. God is the Master Chemist; he knows the exact conditions we need.

In his divine lab, he is producing more than pure compounds, he is forming people of purity, resilience, and radiance, fit for his eternal house. Just as God transforms stones and people, he also works like a master chemist, refining and purifying his people.

ACTIVITY: TOUCH AND CONTEMPLATE — GOD'S WORK IN US

Engage students' senses and imagination by exploring physical samples of stones that illustrate transformation, refinement, and spiritual symbolism discussed in this chapter.

Precious Stones

Materials (easily available on Amazon or rock kit suppliers):

- Raw geode (to break open)
- Obsidian (volcanic glass)
- Petrified wood
- Quartz crystal
- Marble or slate (metamorphic rock)
- Tumbled rock pair (rough and polished versions)

Instructions:

1. Pass around the rocks or display them at a lab station.
2. Examine the texture, weight, and appearance of each.
3. Offer a printed reflection guide (optional) with the following prompt:
   "Each of these stones underwent pressure, time, or fire. Which stone most reflects your current season with God? What is He shaping in you?"

Reflection Examples

- Geode—"There's beauty forming inside, even if others don't see it yet."
- Obsidian—"God brought clarity and sharpness through a sudden trial."
- Petrified wood—"The Spirit's life is quietly filling my structure."
- Marble—"Pressure is refining me below the surface."

REFLECTION QUESTIONS

1. Which image or stone from the chapter (such as geode, obsidian, diamond, or pearl) most resonates with your current spiritual or academic journey? Why? (Consider the transformation each stone underwent—fire, pressure, hidden growth—and how it reflects your own experiences.)

2. How does the metaphor of being "a living stone" shape your understanding of your role within God's house, the church, or your community?

3. What part of your life feels like a "quarry season" where God is quietly shaping you? (How can you embrace this process with hope instead of frustration?)

4. Obsidian forms quickly through upheaval, while marble forms slowly under pressure. Do you tend to grow more through sudden trials or gradual refining? How have you experienced God's hand in either process?

5. What does the idea of "singing stones" or all creation praising God evoke in you? How might you let your life become a form of praise, even in difficult or unseen seasons?

5

Light and Matter
Interaction that Reveals Life

REVEALING THE ATOMIC STRUCTURE

ONE OF THE MOST groundbreaking scientific insights came from studying how light interacts with atoms. Early 20th-century experiments showed that atoms absorb and emit light only at specific energies. When an electron in an atom jumps between energy levels, it absorbs or emits a photon with a precise energy, creating a line spectrum. This line spectrum acts as a unique fingerprint of that element.

Niels Bohr used these observations to develop his atomic model, where electrons orbit the nucleus in discrete energy levels.[1] This model explained the hydrogen atom's spectral lines and laid the foundation for quantum mechanics. Thus, light became a key to unlocking the invisible atomic world.

---

1. Holst, *The Atom and the Bohr Theory*, Kindle edition.

ELECTROMAGNETIC SPECTRUM AND SPECTROSCOPY

Light is part of the electromagnetic spectrum, which includes not only visible light but also radio waves, microwaves, infrared, ultraviolet, X-rays, and gamma rays. Different regions of this spectrum interact with matter in different ways. By studying these interactions, scientists gain invaluable information. This study is called spectroscopy.[2] It is the science of analyzing how matter absorbs, emits, or scatters electromagnetic radiation. Through these techniques, spectroscopy reveals molecular structures, chemical compositions, and physical conditions without destroying the sample.

X-rays, MRI (Magnetic Resonance Imaging), and PET scans rely on electromagnetic interactions to visualize internal body structures. These methods help diagnose diseases without invasive procedures. Certain wavelengths of light, such as those used in photodynamic therapy, activate drugs that kill cancer cells selectively. Spectroscopy detects pollutants and toxins by analyzing light absorption patterns. Through the interaction of light with matter, spectroscopy provides essential insights into drug molecules' structures and behaviors. This molecular-level understanding is fundamental to designing effective and safe medications that improve human health.

LIGHT PRODUCES LIFE: PHOTOSYNTHESIS AND VITAMIN D SYNTHESIS

Beyond revealing the unseen atomic and molecular world, light plays a fundamental role in sustaining life itself. Through photosynthesis, plants capture visible sunlight and convert carbon dioxide and water into glucose and oxygen—a process that forms the base of most food chains on Earth. In this way, light fuels the growth of plants, providing the oxygen we breathe and the energy stored in all living organisms.

---

2. Skoog, *Principles of Instrumental Analysis*, 2018.

Moreover, light enables the synthesis of essential compounds in living beings. For example, ultraviolet (UV) light from the sun triggers the production of vitamin D in human skin, a critical nutrient for bone health and immune function.[3] This natural biochemical reaction shows how light interacts with matter to create molecules vital for our wellbeing.

These processes demonstrate how the interaction between light and matter goes far beyond physics and chemistry—it underpins the very existence and flourishing of life.

INTERACTION OF GOD AS LIGHT WITH HUMANITY

From the very first words of creation, light has been at the heart of God's unfolding story. "Let there be light," God declared (Gen 1:3), and with that command, before anything else took shape, pure, radiant light broke through the formless darkness. This was no ordinary light, it was the very essence of God himself, "God is light, and in him is no darkness at all" (1 John 1:5).

Even the gospel itself is a shining reflection of God's light. As Paul writes in 2 Corinthians 4:6, "Because the God who said, 'Out of darkness light shall shine,' is the One who shined in our hearts to illuminate the knowledge of the glory of God in the face of Jesus Christ." This verse reminds us that the gospel is not just a message but the very light of God breaking into our hearts so that we may know the glory in Christ's face.

Paul reminds us, "For you were once darkness, but now you are light in the LORD. Walk as children of light" (Eph 5:8). To walk as children of light means recognizing that Christ came as life, and his life is our light from within (John 1:4–5). By following him, we will have the light of life (John 8:12). And when we stumble, and we all do, we confess our sins, for he is faithful and righteous to forgive us our sins and cleanse us from all unrighteousness (1 John 1:9). If we walk in the light, we have fellowship with God and with one

---

3. Holick, *Vitamin D*, 2010.

another, and the blood of Jesus his Son cleanses us from every sin (1 John 1:7). Life and light go together as the psalmist wrote: "For with you is the fountain of life; in your light we see light" (Ps 36:9).

This divine enlightenment is vividly illustrated in the account from Luke 24, where Jesus opens the eyes of his disciples to perceive the reality of his resurrection and the fulfillment of Scripture. Initially, the disciples are confused and doubtful, unable to recognize him or fully grasp the events that had taken place:

Two of them were going to a village named Emmaus, talking about all that had happened. Jesus himself came near and walked with them, but their eyes were kept from recognizing him. (Luke 24:13–16). He explained the Scriptures concerning himself, yet they did not understand until later:

> "Then their eyes were opened and they recognized him, and he disappeared from their sight. They asked each other, "Were not our hearts burning within us while he talked with us on the road and opened the Scriptures to us?" (Luke 24:31–32)

This moment powerfully reveals how God's light penetrates our spiritual blindness and awakens our hearts to truth. Just as physical light enables sight, spiritual light from Christ reveals the fullness of God's plan, turning confusion into understanding and despair into hope.

This enlightenment is a gift God desires to give us. Paul prays in Ephesians 1:17–18, "That the God of our LORD Jesus Christ, the glorious Father, may give you the Spirit of wisdom and revelation, so that you may know him better. I pray that the eyes of your heart may be enlightened in order that you may know the hope to which he has called you, the riches of his glorious inheritance in his holy people,"

In ourselves, we have no light. But when we turn our hearts to the LORD (2 Cor 3:17) and touch the true Light, he removes the veil and begins transforming us into his image. The easiest way to come to Jesus is through reading his Word (Ps 119:130) prayerfully, as the word is living and active, shaping and transforming us (Heb 4:12). The light of God's word cleanses us (Eph 5:26), renews our minds (Eph 4:23), transforms our souls (Rom 12:2), and conforms us to the image of his Son (Rom 8:29), leading to our glorification (Rom 8:30). "The path of the righteous is like the light of dawn, which shines brighter and brighter until the full day" (Prov 4:18). As children of light, we are called to shine with the radiance of Christ, so that others may be guided toward the truth and life found in him.

LIGHT ETERNAL: THE PROMISE OF GOD'S GLORY

The Bible begins and ends with light. From the first command—"Let there be light" (Gen 1:3)—to the eternal promise in Revelation, "And night will be no more; they have no need of the light of a lamp or sun, for the LORD God will be their light" (Rev 22:5), light reveals the presence and glory of God.

Here, the physical sources of light—lamps and the sun—are replaced by God himself as the eternal light. This signifies the complete transformation of creation and humanity, mingled perfectly with God. The uncreated Light of God replaces created light, symbolizing the fullness of his presence that illuminates, sustains, and renews all life. The New Jerusalem, then, is not just a city but a redeemed humanity fully united with God, shining with his glory forever.

The New Jerusalem shines with every color of God's glory, an eternal spectrum that reflects the perfect harmony of unity and diversity in his nature and creation. Just as light in science reveals hidden realities and brings life, so God's eternal light illuminates and transforms us, inviting us to walk as his radiant children now and forever.

May we, as children of light, embrace both the wonder of God's creation and the radiant life he offers, reflecting his glory in every color of our unique gifts.

THE DUAL NATURE OF LIGHT AND THE DUAL NATURE OF JESUS

Light, at its core, exhibits a fascinating dual nature: it behaves both as a wave and as a particle. This wave-particle duality challenges our classical understanding of physics and reveals a deeper, more complex reality than what is immediately visible. Light is both observable and measurable, yet it also transcends simple categories.

In a similar way, Jesus embodies a profound dual nature: fully God and fully man. This mystery of incarnation—God made flesh—is a revelation that transcends human logic and understanding. While we can observe the life and teachings of Jesus historically and experientially, his divine nature is revealed through faith and spiritual insight.

Just as the dual nature of light bridges the realms of the seen and unseen, measurable and mysterious, so Jesus bridges the divine and human. Science explores the observable world with instruments and experiments, while faith invites us into the realm of revelation and relationship with God.

This harmony between science and faith invites us to embrace both what we can observe and measure, and what is revealed through God's Spirit. Both realms deepen our understanding of the world and the One who created it.

ACTIVITY: THE FLAME TEST

A simple yet striking demonstration of how light interacts with matter is the flame test. When a metal salt solution is sprayed into a flame, the metal's electrons absorb energy and jump to a higher energy level, known as an excited state. If you think electrons are shy, just watch them jump excitedly in the flame test; they can't wait to glow! However, this excited state is unstable, and the electrons quickly return to their original, lower energy level, called the ground state. As they return, the energy they gained is released in the form of light, which is referred to as emission. The color of the emitted light depends on the metal: potassium produces a lilac color, calcium emits a crimson red, sodium gives off a bright yellow, and copper shines with a vibrant green. This simple experiment shows that science reveals the unique "light" and identity God has given each element, reflecting his creative order and diversity in the natural world.

This simple display of light's interaction with matter is a vivid reminder of the unique identity and creativity God has woven into every element of creation.

Procedure:

This experiment demonstrates how light interacts with matter at the atomic level by observing the characteristic colors produced when different metal ions are heated in a flame.

Materials Needed

- Bunsen burner or a clean gas flame source
- Nichrome or platinum wire loop (or a clean metal wire)
- Samples of metal salts (e.g., potassium chloride, calcium chloride, sodium chloride, copper (II) chloride)
- Safety goggles and lab coat

Safety Precautions

- Wear safety goggles and a lab coat at all times.
- Handle acids carefully and use in a well-ventilated area.
- Keep flammable materials away from the flame.
- Perform the test under supervision if in a classroom.

Steps

- Dip the clean wire loop into the solid metal salt sample or into a solution of the metal salt, ensuring a small amount of the sample sticks to the loop.
- Place the wire loop with the sample into the hottest part of the Bunsen burner flame (usually the tip of the inner blue cone).
- Observe the color of the flame carefully as the sample heats.
- Record the color observed for each metal salt tested.
- After each test, clean the wire loop by dipping it in hydrochloric acid and heating it in the flame until no color appears. This prevents contamination between samples.

REFLECTION QUESTIONS

1. What does it mean to you personally that "God is light, and in him there is no darkness at all" (1 John 1:5)? How does this truth influence your understanding of God's character and your relationship with him?

2. How does the call to "walk as children of light" (Eph 5:8) challenge or encourage you in your daily life? In what ways can you reflect God's light to others?

3. Considering the scientific examples we explored—such as photosynthesis, vitamin D synthesis, and the flame test—how does light reveal hidden realities in nature? How does this deepen your appreciation of God as the Creator who reveals truth and sustains life?

4. Have you experienced moments when God's Word or Spirit has illuminated your heart and changed how you "conduct" yourself in the world? Can you describe how this inner transformation has affected your attitudes, choices, or relationships?

5. How do the physical properties of light and its spiritual symbolism together help you understand the harmony between God's creation and his presence in your life?

6

The Rhythm of Rest
Sabbath and the Whisper of God

IN OUR HURRIED WORLD, the presence of God can seem distant, drowned out by constant motion, noise, and distraction. But from the very beginning, God invited us into a different pace, a rhythm of life woven not in urgency, but in trust. He wrote rest into the very fabric of creation. Sabbath is not simply a pause from work; it is a return to our source, a reconnection with the One who made us.

The first time the Bible mentions rest is in Genesis 2:2: "By the seventh day God had finished the work he had been doing; so on the seventh day he rested from all his work." But what is truly striking is that humanity's first full day was God's day of rest. Before Adam tilled the ground or named a single creature, his first sunrise unfolded not in labor, but in stillness. His first breath was drawn in a world already complete. He began not with performance, but with presence. This is the rhythm of grace: life begins with God's work—not ours.

Under the old covenant, the Sabbath was a day to cease. Under the new covenant, it becomes a Person in whom we abide. Jesus is not merely LORD of the Sabbath; he is the Sabbath. His finished work on the cross is the deepest rest we will ever know.

The Rhythm of Rest

In him, we rest from striving, from shame, from the exhausting need to prove our worth. In him, our work flows from rest, not toward it. Sabbath is loving the LORD with our whole being. As Paul writes, "It is no longer I who live, but Christ who lives in me" (Gal 2:20). That is Sabbath. " . . . yet not I but the grace of God" (1 Cor 15:10), and that is Sabbath. Sabbath is looking away from ourselves and looking to Jesus. It is trusting him, abiding in him, and allowing him to be our Shepherd, our Life, and our Rest.

To pray is Sabbath. To cast our burdens on him is Sabbath. Sabbath becomes more than a moment; it becomes a rhythm, a way of moving through life that trusts God's strength over our own.

Seen through this lens, the natural world is not just a testimony to God's creative power, it is a place to meet him, to receive him, and to rest in what he has already done. Creation becomes a kind of invitation, drawing us into the deeper reality of Sabbath: not a day, but a life hidden in Christ.

When we live in that rhythm, we step out of the rush and into the quiet testimony of creation. We join the heavens in declaring the glory of God. We join the earth in revealing his handiwork. Sabbath rest opens our eyes and ears to the divine symphony playing all around us.

Even scientists, knowingly or not, have testified to this intricate beauty. Francis Bacon once said that to study nature is to glorify the Creator.[1] Werner Heisenberg[2] echoed this awe: "The first gulp from the glass of natural sciences will turn you into an atheist, but at the bottom of the glass God is waiting for you."

The deeper we look, the more we see that beauty is not accidental. Precision is not random. The rhythm of rest, the architecture of atoms, the orbit of stars, all of it points not only to power, but to presence.

Scripture affirms this truth. As Romans 1:20 declares, "For since the creation of the world God's invisible qualities, his eternal power and divine nature, have been clearly seen, being understood

---

1. Scott and Vare, "Francis Bacon and the Interrogation of Nature."
2. Heisenberg, *Physics and Philosophy*.

from what has been made." Nature is not silent; it is a living witness, a sermon without words, revealing the eternal attributes of God.

When we step outside we enter a living sanctuary not adorned with stained glass and pews but with skies and trees, wind, and waves. The breeze whispers his gentleness. The oceans roar his might. The trees lift their limbs like hands raised in praise. In this sacred space creation becomes a temple not built by human hands but spoken into being by the word himself. Here we are invited not just to observe but to behold, to listen and to respond.

So, as you read these words, let this be a Sabbath moment for your soul. Step out of the noise. Pause. Look. Listen. The heavens are declaring his glory, and he is inviting you to rest in him.

Sabbath is not a day; it is a way of being.

It is the deep soul-rest that comes from knowing the work is finished, the striving is over, and that we are baptized into him, into his death (Rom 6:3). We are crucified with him, and it is no longer we who live (Gal 2:20); our life is now hidden with Christ in God (Col 3:3). We are grafted into him (Rom 11:19), and we abide in him, and he abides in us (John 15:4–5).

To live in Sabbath is to live from his strength instead of our own, to walk not by effort but by trust. Creation still echoes this invitation to cease from anxious striving and abide in the sufficiency of Christ. It is about rejoicing in the LORD and the peace of God, guarding our hearts and minds in Christ Jesus.

The wind still whispers his gentleness. The heavens still declare his glory. The trees still reach in silent praise. And in all of it, God is still speaking—calling us to dwell, to behold, and to rest in him . . . moment by moment, breath by breath.

MEDITATION: FROM CREATION TO CHRIST — KNOWING GOD THROUGH WHAT HE HAS MADE

In the busyness of campus life, it's easy to rush past the trees, the wind, the stars. treating them as scenery, not sacred space. But Scripture reminds us that creation is not mute. It declares. It proclaims. It reveals. If we slow down and pay attention, we begin to hear a deeper voice, a voice that speaks not just of nature, but of God.

This next section offers a series of short meditations designed to help you do just that: pause, look, and listen. Each day draws from Scripture and creation, helping you trace the fingerprints of Christ from the heavens to the earth, and ultimately to your own heart. You don't need special tools, only a quiet spirit and a willingness to see again.

Day 1: Joining Heaven and Earth in Praise

Psalm 19:1-2 The heavens declare the glory of God; the skies proclaim the work of his hands. Day after day they pour forth speech; night after night they reveal knowledge.

Isaiah 45:18 He who created the heavens . . . He founded [the earth]; He did not create it to be empty, but formed it to be inhabited.

Lift your eyes. The heavens are not silent—they pour forth praise. The skies are God's canopy, spread out with majesty, drawing our gaze upward to worship. The earth below stands firm, intentionally formed to be a home for life. This world is no accident but a sacred space—God's sanctuary—inviting us to pause, behold, and find our place within his grand design. All of creation, seen and unseen, holds together in Christ, who is before all things and through whom all things were made (Col 1:16-17).

Day 2: Moon and Stars, His Fingerprints

Psalm 8:3-4 When I consider your heavens, the work of your fingers, the moon and the stars . . . what is mankind that you are mindful of them?

Job 38:31 Can you bind the chains of the Pleiades or loose the cords of Orion's belt?

The stars are not random sparks scattered in the dark; they are the fingerprints of God, carefully named and placed by his hand. The galaxies spin in silent worship, following his perfect order. Yet, the same God who orchestrates the vast cosmos is intimately mindful of you. As you gaze into the night sky, remember the prophetic word is like a lamp shining in the darkness—guiding your heart until the morning star rises within you, illuminating your path and revealing that you are deeply known and cherished by the Creator (2 Pet 1:19).

Day 3: Faithfulness in Every Sunrise

Ecclesiastes 1:5–6 The sun rises and the sun sets . . . The wind blows to the south and turns to the north; round and round it goes.

Genesis 8:22 As long as the earth endures, seedtime and harvest, cold and heat, summer and winter . . . will never cease.

Creation's cycles mirror the spiritual truth: just as seedtime and harvest faithfully follow one another, so does the word of God planted in our hearts grow and bear abundant fruit. The sun rises and sets, the seasons turn, and God's faithfulness never ceases. In this divine rhythm, our hearts are the soil, the word the seed, and the Spirit the life-giving rain, nurturing us to produce a harvest a hundredfold (Mark 4).

Day 4: Clothed in His Care

Matthew 6:26 Look at the birds . . . they do not sow or reap . . . yet your heavenly Father feeds them.

Matthew 6:28–29 See how the flowers . . . grow. They do not labor or spin. Yet . . . not even Solomon . . . was dressed like one of these.

The birds do not worry, and the lilies do not strive—yet they are sustained in beauty and grace. Their lives are marked by quiet trust, simply being what God made them to be. In their rest, we are invited to find our own. You are worth more than many sparrows.

Let creation teach you to trust the faithful care of your Father, who knows what you need before you even ask.

Day 5: Christ, the Shepherd of Our Soul

Psalm 23:1-3 The LORD is my shepherd; I shall not want. He maketh me to lie down in green pastures; he leadeth me beside the still waters. He restoreth my soul . . .

John 10:11 I am the good shepherd. The good shepherd lays down his life for the sheep.

The One who hung the stars also walks beside you as your Shepherd. He leads with tenderness, restores with presence, and guards with his own life. Just as creation reflects his care in every sunrise and sparrow, so our hearts find rest when we follow his voice. In Christ, we are not lost in the vastness—we are known, guided, and deeply loved.

Day 6: Resting in Christ, the LORD of All Creation

Hebrews 4:9-10 There remains, then, a Sabbath-rest for the people of God; for anyone who enters God's rest also rests from their works, just as God did from his.

Matthew 11:28-30 Come to me, all you who are weary and burdened, and I will give you rest . . . For my yoke is easy and my burden is light.

Creation began with rest—not as an afterthought, but as the foundation. In the same way, the life of faith begins not with striving, but with receiving. Christ, the Creator, invites us into his finished work, just as Adam began his life in the rest of God. To walk with him is to live from rest, not toward it, yoked to grace, not burdened by effort. Here, in Christ, we dwell in a rest that no season can shake and no striving can earn.

A WEEK IN THE RHYTHM OF REST

True Sabbath is more than a day—it is a Person. Jesus, the LORD of the Sabbath, offers rest not only for our bodies but for our souls. He invites us to lay down what we were never meant to carry, to stop striving for what cannot be earned, and to live fully in the sufficiency of his grace.

Resting in Christ means trusting that his work is enough. It means trading anxiety for peace, weariness for strength, and performance for presence. This is not the rest of escape—it is the rest of communion. A steady rhythm of abiding in the One who holds all things together.

Creation still moves in this rhythm, and so can we. In Christ, we return to the original harmony of Eden—walking with God in the cool of the day, no longer driven by effort, but drawn by love. He is our Rest, our Refuge, and our Redeemer.

So pause. Breathe. Dwell. Let the stillness of creation draw your soul to the Savior. Let the glory of the skies and the gentleness of the sparrow remind you: he is near, and he is enough.

FROM WONDER TO LOVE: TURNING TO THE ONE BEHIND IT ALL

After a week of beholding creation as sacred space—filled with God's glory, rhythm, and rest—we now turn to the One whom creation reflects. Nature stirs wonder, but Jesus brings transformation. The heavens declare the glory of God, but it is in Christ that his heart is fully revealed.

This week, we move from awe to intimacy. From watching the sunrise to walking with the Son. These daily reflections invite you to meet the LORD not just as Creator, but as Shepherd, Physician, and Friend. He draws near. He speaks. He restores.

Let your heart now turn fully to him—Jesus, the Living Word, the One who walks with you, loves you, and transforms you from glory to glory.

The Rhythm of Rest

Day 1: He Walks With Us When We Are Down

Luke 24:17 He asked them, "What are you discussing together as you walk along?" They stood still, their faces downcast.

Luke 24:32 They asked each other, "Were not our hearts burning within us while he talked with us on the road and opened the Scriptures to us?"

When we are downcast, confused, or grieving, Jesus draws near. On the road to Emmaus, the risen LORD joined two disciples in their sorrow, not with instant answers, but with gentle presence. He walked with them, listened to their hearts, and opened the Scriptures to reveal himself. At the table, when he broke the bread, their eyes were opened, they recognized him. This is who he is: the One who meets us in our lowest moments, walking with us even when we don't see him. Through the word, he unveils his heart. In our fellowship with him, he makes himself known. And in his nearness, sorrow gives way to burning hope. Don't be afraid to tell him what's troubling you; your fears, your burdens, your hidden cares. He himself is the answer your heart is looking for.

Day 2: Just Love Him—Everything Will Be Alright

John 21:3 I'm going out to fish," Simon Peter told them . . . but that night they caught nothing.

John 21:17 The third time he said to him, 'Simon son of John, do you love me?' . . . Jesus said, 'Feed my sheep.'"

Peter found himself weary and disoriented. He returned to fishing, back to what he knew. But even there, Jesus came to him. He didn't rebuke him; he fed him, restored him, and asked only one question: "Do you love me?" Jesus doesn't need your perfection. He simply wants your heart. When we say, "LORD, you know I love you," everything else begins to fall into place. Love for him becomes the reason we rise, serve, and keep going. Just love him—he will meet you there, restore your soul, and gently lead you forward.

Day 3: He Is the Shepherd of Your Soul

1 Peter 2:25 . . . but now you have returned to the Shepherd and Overseer of your souls."

Psalm 23:1–3 The LORD is my shepherd, I lack nothing. He makes me lie down in green pastures, He leads me beside quiet waters, He refreshes my soul."

Our souls need constant care. We are easily burdened—restless in thought, weary in heart, scattered by worry. But Jesus is the Shepherd of our soul. He doesn't just guide our steps—he tends to the deepest parts of us. As vulnerable sheep, we often drift toward anxiety or try to carry life alone. But the Shepherd calls us to lie down, to be still, to let him lead. In him, we lack nothing. He knows how to restore what's been worn down and to quiet what feels unsettled. Let him care for your soul today—gently, faithfully, and fully. Return to him. He knows just what you need.

Day 4: Do Not Miss Him in His Word

John 5:39–40 You study the Scriptures diligently because you think that in them you have eternal life. These are the very Scriptures that testify about me, yet you refuse to come to me to have life.

Colossians 3:16 Let the message of Christ dwell among you richly . . .

It's possible to read the Bible and still miss the One it reveals. Jesus reminds us that the Scriptures lead us to him, the Living Word. His words are not just to be studied, but received as spirit and life. Like a cow chewing the cud, we're invited to linger with his word, letting it sink deep through prayer and reflection. As we return to him in the word, he dwells in us, not just with knowledge, but with presence. Turn your hearts to him. Speak to him. Drink the living water. Let the word of Christ dwell in you richly.

Day 5: Invite Him into Your Boat

Matthew 8:24-27 Suddenly a furious storm came up on the lake . . . But Jesus was sleeping. The disciples went and woke him, saying, 'LORD, save us! We're going to drown!' . . . Then he got up and rebuked the winds and the waves, and it was completely calm.

Life often feels like a stormy sea, waves rising, winds howling, fears pressing in. But if Jesus is in the boat, you are not alone. The disciples were overwhelmed, yet Jesus was already with them, calm, present, and fully in control. Don't fix your eyes on the storm; fix them on him. Even when he seems silent, he is not distant. He is the One whom even the wind and waves obey. Invite him into every part of your journey, especially the uncertain, fearful places. Look away from the chaos, and unto him, the Author and Perfecter of your faith. His presence brings peace, even in the middle of the storm. Trust him.

Day 6: Don't Miss the Moment

Matthew 12:50 For whoever does the will of my Father in heaven is my brother and sister and mother.

Colossians 1:9b We continually ask God to fill you with the knowledge of his will through all the wisdom and understanding that the Spirit gives.

Every situation in life, whether joyful or difficult, is never random. The LORD is sovereign and purposeful in all he allows. In his hands, each moment becomes an invitation to seek his will, know his heart, and grow in intimacy with him. We have been joined to the LORD, made one spirit with him. As we abide in him and he abides in us, we begin to see that apart from him, we can do nothing. Yet in him, even the smallest act becomes fruitful. As we fix our gaze on him, we are being transformed, bit by bit, from glory to glory, reflecting more of who he is. So don't rush past today. Pause. Listen. Let your steps align with his heart. His will is not a burden, but a blessing—good, pleasing, and perfect.

ACTIVITY: SOAP-MAKING AND THE RHYTHM OF SABBATH

To embody this truth, we will enter a simple, quiet space of creation—a soap-making activity. In this process, we mix oil and sodium hydroxide (lye), and then we wait. Once these ingredients combine, a reaction called saponification begins. It is invisible to the eye, yet completely reliable. The soap forms not because we force it to, but because the ingredients have been designed to respond to one another. This is not striving; it is trust. The transformation happens because the reaction obeys the chemical laws. This becomes a picture of Sabbath, and of grace.

Like soap-making, the life of faith is not about striving to make something happen. Sabbath is not earning. It is resting in what God has already done. Grace, like Sabbath, teaches us to stop, trust, and receive. In Christ, the work is finished. The transformation is his.

We prepare, we pour, and we wait—not anxiously, but confidently. The soap will come. So will the fruit in our lives as we abide in him.

Materials Needed

- Coconut oil—100.0 g
- Sodium hydroxide (NaOH) solution—38.0 mL (11.4 M; prepared by dissolving 17.3 g NaOH in 38 mL water)
  Note: When preparing sodium hydroxide solution, always add NaOH slowly to water while cooling to prevent overheating.
- Essential oil (optional, for fragrance)
- 500 mL beaker
- Graduated cylinder
- Magnetic stir bar or glass stirring rod
- Hot plate or slow cooker
- Spatula (optional)

- Soap mold or tray
- Gloves (CAUTION: Sodium hydroxide is caustic—always wear gloves when handling)
- pH test strips

Procedure

1. Place 100.0 g of coconut oil into a 500 mL beaker. Heat gently on a hot plate or slow cooker until it reaches 40–45°C.
2. Measure 38.0 mL of sodium hydroxide (NaOH) solution (11.4 M). Slowly add the sodium hydroxide solution to the heated coconut oil while stirring continuously with a magnetic stir bar or glass rod.
3. Stir constantly until the mixture thickens and reaches the "trace" stage. To check for trace, dip a spatula into the mixture and lift it—if the drips leave a faint trail or line on the surface, trace has been reached.
4. (Optional) Add a few drops of essential oil for fragrance and stir gently to combine.
5. Carefully pour the soap mixture into a mold or tray.
6. Allow the soap to cure for 4–6 weeks. This curing time hardens the soap and completes the saponification process.
7. After curing, test the pH of the soap with pH test strips. The safe pH range for skin contact is 8–10.

7

A Man According to God's Heart
Delighting in God and His Word

To know God is the highest calling of the human soul. From the beginning, he created us not merely to exist, but to live in fellowship with him, to know his ways, love his heart, and walk in his truth. The Scriptures reveal that this knowledge is not only an exercise of the mind but a posture of the whole person, heart, soul, and strength. In this way, it is much like the pursuit of science. A scientist does not come to understand the natural world through casual glances, but through patient observation, disciplined inquiry, and deep wonder at its intricacies. In the same way, we come to know God not by fleeting interest but by sustained attention to his word and his works. The heavens declare his glory, and the pages of Scripture unveil his heart. Together, they invite us into the fullness of truth.

From the very beginning, humanity was created for intimate fellowship with God. Made in his image (Gen 1:27), man was declared "very good" by God (Gen 1:31). With man now on the earth, God's work of creation was complete, and he rested (Gen 2:2).

Man's creation was unique among all living things. God "breathed into his nostrils the breath of life, and the man became a living being" (Gen 2:7). He placed man in the garden of Eden, where "the tree of life" stood at its center (Gen 2:9), symbolizing the divine life God intended for him to enjoy.

From the earliest days, humanity's highest privilege has been to call upon the name of the LORD. In the time of Enosh, "people began to call on the name of the LORD" (Gen 4:26), establishing a practice that would endure throughout generations as a defining mark of those who know and follow him (Job 12:4; Gen 12:8; Gen 21:33; Deut. 4:7; Judg 15:18; 1 Sam 12:18; 2 Sam 22:4; Ps 99:6). In times of prosperity, it became an expression of gratitude (Ps 105:1; Isa 12:3-4); in seasons of distress, it rose as a plea for deliverance (Ps 50:15; Ps 91:15). To call on his name was to acknowledge his nearness (Jer. 29:12), to rely on his covenant faithfulness (Zeph 3:9; Zech 13:9), and to partake in his life-giving presence, an act both commanded by God (Ps 50:15; Jer 29:12) and treasured by him (Ps 91:15).

Enoch walked with God and was taken into his presence without experiencing death (Gen 5:22). Noah found favor in the eyes of God (Gen 6:8), entered into a covenant with him (Gen 6:18), and after the flood, he built an altar to God in worship (Gen 8:20).

This pattern of fellowship continued in the life of Abraham. When God appeared to him, Abraham built an altar there to God who had appeared to him (Gen 12:7) and called on the name of God (Gen 12:8). God revealed himself to Abraham as his shield and his very great reward (Gen 15:1) and as God Almighty (Gen 17:1)

God's love for man reached even the level of human friendship. In Genesis 18, he visited Abraham in human form, eating with him and speaking face to face. Later, Abraham planted a tamarisk tree in Beersheba where he called on the name of God, the Eternal God (Gen 21:33).

Through the prophet Zechariah, God described his people in the most intimate terms: for whoever touches you touches the apple of his eye (Zech 2:8). His love is steadfast and everlasting: I have loved you with an everlasting love; I have drawn you with unfailing kindness (Jer 31:3).

Throughout Scripture, God expresses his love for humanity in tender ways. He is not only Creator but also husband: For your Maker is your husband; the LORD Almighty is his name (Isa 54:5). And I will betroth you to me forever (Hos 2:19). He remembers with affection the life in the wilderness of his people: I remember the devotion of your youth, how as a bride you loved me and followed through the wilderness (Jer 2:2). From the very beginning, God's deepest desire for humanity has been love, a love that flows from the very center of who we are. When Moses stood before Israel and declared, Love the LORD your God with all your heart and with all your soul and with all your strength (Deut 6:5), he voiced God's longing for his people.

SOLOMON'S SONG OF SONGS: THE INTIMATE LOVE BETWEEN GOD AND MAN

The Song of Songs (1–8) portrays the progressive, personal, and spiritual journey of a believer's relationship with God. This book uniquely expresses the intimate love between God and his seekers, which can also be understood as the bridal love between Christ, the bridegroom, and his followers, the bride. A lover of God is drawn by his affection, pursuing him for complete satisfaction and growing in maturity throughout the relationship. The emphasis is on the love exchanged between believers and the LORD—God revealing himself as the beloved, and the seeker responding as his beloved. Through his wisdom, God fulfills his eternal purpose in divine love, inviting us into deeper fellowship and ultimate oneness with him.

DAVID'S LOVE FOR GOD AND HIS WORD

God's desire for intimate relationship with his people extends beyond longing for love, it includes calling them to treasure his word as the guiding and sustaining force of their lives. Among all the figures in the Old Testament shaped by God's word, David shines as a man after God's own heart. His life, though marked by trials, betrayals, and personal failures, was anchored in a deep affection for the LORD and his law. This love is nowhere more visible than in the psalms David wrote, songs that still lift the hearts of believers today.

David did not merely know God's word; he delighted in it. His psalms overflow with awe at God's wisdom and goodness. In Psalm 16:11, David declares, "You make known to me the path of life; you will fill me with joy in your presence, with eternal pleasures at your right hand." For David, God's word was not a list of rules but a path to life itself, a way into God's own presence where true joy is found.

The title of Psalm 18 tells us that David sang it to the LORD after being delivered from all his enemies and from Saul. He opens with a simple yet profound confession: "I love You, LORD, my strength." These were not empty words but the testimony of a man who had seen God's hand in battle, in hardship, and in the quiet moments of life.

In Psalm 19:7-10, David pours out praise for God's law, describing it as perfect, reviving the soul; trustworthy, making the simple wise; and radiant, bringing joy to the heart. To him, the Scriptures were more valuable than pure gold and sweeter than fresh honey, a treasure to cherish and a delight to taste.

David's songs reveal the depth of his relationship with God. In Psalm 22, he clings to the LORD in trust even amid suffering. In Psalm 23, he paints the timeless portrait of God as the Shepherd who leads, restores, and protects even through life's darkest valleys, reminding us of his continual presence and sustaining power. Psalm 37:4 captures David's posture of delight: "Take delight in the LORD and he will give you the desires of your heart." This was not about selfish desires but about aligning his heart so closely with God's will that his longings matched the LORD's own.

David's love for God's word was not separate from his love for God himself. In Psalm 40:8, he declares, "I desire to do your will, my God; your law is within my heart." God's truth had sunk so deeply into him that it became part of who he was. And in Psalm

43:4, he celebrates God as his joy and delight, longing to go to the altar of God with a heart ready to praise.

For David, loving God meant loving his word. It was his source of wisdom, comfort, and joy. It shaped his prayers, guided his choices, and steadied him in both triumph and trouble. To read David's psalms is to see a man whose heartbeat in rhythm with God's voice, a reminder that to love the LORD is to treasure every word he speaks.

JOSHUA: A FAITHFUL LEADER ROOTED IN GOD'S WORD

Joshua, chosen to lead Israel into the Promised Land, stands as a powerful example of a man who delighted in God and his word. When God commanded him, "Keep this Book of the Law always on your lips; meditate on it day and night," (Joshua 1:8a), it was a call to root his leadership in constant reflection on God's promises and commands. Long before this, Joshua and Caleb boldly encouraged the people to trust God's provision, reminding them that the land was good and that "but the LORD is with us. Do not be afraid of them." (Num 14:6–9). Throughout his leadership, Joshua urged the people to cling tightly to the LORD and to love him wholeheartedly (Josh 23:8–11). His life teaches us that true success comes not from human strength or strategy alone but from a heart deeply connected to God, sustained by steady delight in his Word.

NEHEMIAH: A LEADER ACCORDING TO GOD'S HEART

Nehemiah was an ordinary Jewish man living in exile, serving as cupbearer to the king in Babylon. Though far from Jerusalem, his heart remained deeply connected to God's purposes for his people. When he heard the devastating news that the walls of Jerusalem were broken down and its gates burned with fire (Neh

1:3), Nehemiah was moved to profound grief, he wept, mourned, fasted, and prayed earnestly (1:4). This was not just a moment of sorrow but a turning point that stirred him to action.

Recognizing the critical need for restoration, Nehemiah took courageous leadership to rebuild the city walls. But his vision went beyond physical reconstruction. He understood that true revival begins with the word of God. So, he brought Ezra the scribe to read the Law of Moses aloud to the people. From dawn until midday, men and women alike listened attentively to God's words, and the power of Scripture stirred their hearts deeply, causing many to weep (Neh 8:3-9).

Yet Nehemiah encouraged the people not to be overcome by grief. Instead, he reminded them, "Go and enjoy choice food and sweet drinks . . . This day is holy to our LORD. Do not grieve, for the joy of the LORD is your strength." (Neh 8:10). This joy, rooted in God's presence, became their source of strength.

For days, the Law was read and celebrated, culminating in a solemn assembly on the eighth day that marked a renewed covenant with God and a community committed to living by his word (8:18). Nehemiah's example teaches us that delighting in God and his word fuels both spiritual revival and practical action. It shows how a heart devoted to God's promises can bring restoration and hope even in the most broken circumstances.

EATING THE WORD TO BE JOYFUL

From the earliest pages of Scripture, God calls his people not only to obey his word but to love it deeply. His word is meant to be more than rules on a page; it is life-giving, sustaining, and sweet.

Jeremiah understood this. He speaks of finding God's words and eating them, describing them as the joy and delight of his heart (Jer 15:16). For Jeremiah, God's word was not just instruction, it was nourishment to his soul, filling him with gladness even in the midst of difficulty.

Ezekiel had a similar encounter. In Ezekiel 3:1-3, God commands him, "Son of man, eat what is before you; eat this scroll; then go and speak to the people of Israel." Ezekiel obeyed, and as he ate the scroll filled with God's words, he found it "as sweet as honey" in his mouth. This vivid imagery speaks to the nourishment that Scripture provides. Just as food sustains the body, God's word sustains the soul. It is sweet to those who receive it with faith, bringing delight even in seasons of challenge.

DANIEL'S UNDERSTANDING OF SCRIPTURE: FAITHFULNESS IN EXILE

Daniel's heart belonged fully to God. From the beginning of his life in Babylon, he resolved not to defile himself with the king's food or wine, choosing obedience over compromise (Dan 1:8). His faithfulness was unwavering, even when threatened with death, as he and his friends refused to bow to the golden image, declaring to the king that they would serve no other god (Dan 3:18). Because Daniel treasured God's word and lived by it, God used him in significant ways.

One day, while reading the writings of the prophet Jeremiah, Daniel discovered that God had decreed seventy years of captivity for Israel, after which he would restore his people to their land. Realizing the time of fulfillment was near, Daniel turned to God with fasting, prayer, and confession, seeking his mercy and guidance for the nation. This act of devotion positioned him as a vessel through whom God would bring about the transition from exile to the return to the land of promise.

God regarded Daniel with deep affection. More than once, heavenly messengers addressed him as "man of preciousness" (Dan 10:11, 19). When Daniel prayed, the answer from heaven was swift, for God valued his heart and faithfulness. At the beginning of his supplications, the command was given, and an angel came to tell him that he was precious in God's sight, urging him to understand the vision (Dan 9:23). Daniel's life shows that those who love God's word and seek him earnestly become channels for his purposes on earth.

LIKE A BEE WITH HONEY: ATTENTIVE AND PERSISTENT BIBLE READING

The bee does not rush. It does not panic. It goes from flower to flower with calm focus, collecting nectar one drop at a time. It doesn't gather much in a single trip, but over time, through thousands of flights, it produces honey: sweet, nourishing, and enduring.

Likewise, reading the Bible should not be hurried or mechanical. In a world of skimming and scrolling, we're invited to read like bees, attentively, persistently, and quietly in a prayerful manner. We gather truth and wisdom little by little, day after day. Though it may not seem like much at first, over time it becomes something beautiful: insight, strength, joy, and a life that reflects God's nature.

Bees are not loud or showy. They work quietly, often unseen, but their labor is essential. So it is with our time in God's word. We may not always have dramatic experiences, but each moment spent reading and meditating on Scripture builds something deep within us.

Let us learn from the bee: to read slowly, gather deeply, and let the sweetness of God's word nourish us from the inside out.

LIKE A COW CHEWING CUD: RETURNING TO THE WORD AGAIN AND AGAIN

Cows have four stomachs, and their digestion process is slow and deliberate. They chew their food, swallow it, and then bring it back up to chew again, rechewing, digesting it more deeply each time. This isn't a sign of inefficiency but of thoroughness. The cow takes its time, drawing every bit of nourishment from what it eats.

In the same way, meditating on Scripture means we don't just read once and move on. We return to it. We chew it slowly, reflecting, praying, asking questions, sometimes even memorizing. We may revisit the same passage several times over days or even years, and each time God feeds us something new.

This kind of Bible reading might feel less productive in the moment than checking off a chapter a day, but like the cow, we draw deep spiritual nourishment. As Psalm 1 says, the one who meditates on the word "day and night" becomes like a tree planted by streams of water, fruitful, resilient, and flourishing.

Choose one verse a day to chew on like a cow this week, read it each day, pray it back to God, write it out, or discuss it with a friend. You'll be surprised how much nourishment God can bring from a single bite, slowly savored.

LONGING FOR GOD'S PRESENCE: A FOUNDATION FOR INTELLECTUAL AND SPIRITUAL ENGAGEMENT

From the very core of our being, we are created to seek God. He is the One our soul longs for, whose love surpasses every earthly pursuit. This longing is not a fleeting feeling but a deep desire to live in fellowship with the Creator, to know his ways, and to walk in step with his heart. As the seeker in Scripture prays, "Place me like a seal on your heart, like a seal on your arm; for love is as strong as death . . . " It burns like blazing fire, like a mighty flame" (Song 8:6), we too are called to approach God's word with the determination not to miss him in its pages.

For the student of science, this longing finds a unique expression. The same God who authored the Scriptures also designed the intricate order of the natural world. Every equation, reaction, and biological process reflects his creativity and wisdom. Just as a scientist observes with careful attention to uncover hidden patterns, so a believer searches the Scriptures to discover the heart and mind of God. In both pursuits, curiosity is rewarded with deeper understanding, and humility is essential, because truth is never our invention but always God's revelation.

As the LORD says, "Heaven is my throne, and the earth is my footstool . . . These are the ones I look on with favor: those who are humble and contrite in spirit, and who tremble at my word" (Isa 66:1–2). In science, humility acknowledges the limits of our knowledge; in faith, humility bows before the One whose knowledge has no limit. Both realms invite us to keep our hearts teachable, ready to be corrected, expanded, and transformed by truth—whether revealed through creation or through the Word.

KNOWING GOD AND HIS WAYS MEANS LOVING HIM AND HIS WORD

To truly know God and understand his ways is to love him and delight in his word. Scripture teaches that knowledge of God is not merely intellectual but relational—a heart drawn toward him in love and obedience. Loving God with all our heart, soul, and strength (Deut 6:5) leads us to cherish his word, which reveals his character, will, and promises. As we meditate on it day and night (Ps 1:2), we grow in intimate knowledge of God that transforms our lives and aligns us with his divine purposes.

ACTIVITY: A LOVING SEEKER OF THE WORD—PSALM 119 REFLECTION

Throughout this chapter, we've explored how the word of God shaped the lives and leadership of key Old Testament figures. We now turn to Psalm 119, a profound meditation on God's word, to help us reflect personally on the psalmist's attitudes and apply them to their own academic and spiritual journeys.

Selected Verses from Psalm 119

- *Psalm 119:2*—"Blessed are those who keep his testimonies, who seek him with all their heart."
- *Psalm 119:66*—"Teach me proper discernment and knowledge, for I believe in your commandments."
- *Psalm 119:30*—"I have chosen the way of faithfulness; your ordinances I have set before me."

- *Psalm 119:73*—"Let your hand be ready to help me, for I have chosen Your precepts."
- *Psalm 119:48*—"I will lift up my hands to Your commandments, which I love, and I will meditate on your statutes."
- *Psalm 119:103*—"How sweet are your words to my taste, sweeter than honey to my mouth!"
- *Psalm 119:54*—"Your statutes have been my songs in the house of my pilgrimage."
- *Psalm 119:80*—"May my heart be blameless in your statutes, so that I will not be ashamed."
- *Psalm 119:36*—"Incline my heart to your testimonies and not to selfish gain."

Reflection Questions

- Please read through the verses and identify one or two key phrases or attitudes that stand out in the psalmist's relationship with God's Word.

Additional Questions:

- How does the chapter describe the unique relationship between God and humanity from creation onward? In what ways can you cultivate that kind of intimate fellowship with God in your own life?
- David's deep love for God's Word shaped his life, even in trials and failures. How can you relate to David's example of delighting in Scripture as a source of strength and guidance? Can you share a time when God's Word comforted or directed you?
- The chapter highlights the importance of meditating on Scripture "like a bee gathering nectar" and "like a cow

chewing cud." What does this teach you about how you might approach your own Bible reading and study? How could this method impact your spiritual growth?

- Leaders like Joshua and Nehemiah modeled delighting in God's Word as foundational for their leadership and community restoration. How might delighting in God's Word influence your approach to leadership, study, or future vocation?

- The chapter emphasizes that loving God involves loving his Word as the path to truly know him. How can you cultivate a deeper love and delight for Scripture in your daily routine, especially when academic or life pressures make it challenging?

8

Building on the Rock
A Life Anchored in the Word

MEET THE MAN

AT THE HEART OF the journey for anyone who delights deeply in God and treasures his word stands a singular, glorious fulfillment: Jesus Christ himself. From the moment of his baptism, when the Father's voice thundered, "This is my beloved Son, with whom I am well pleased," to the radiant glory revealed on the mount of transfiguration, Jesus was affirmed as the Father's delight, completely aligned with God's will. He loved the Father with a deep, unwavering devotion, often sending away the crowd so he could spend quiet moments alone in prayer and intimate communion with him.

In the Gospel of John, Jesus declares that he speaks nothing on his own but only does what the Father commands. He does not seek to glorify himself but lives wholly submitted to the Father's will. He came as the Good Shepherd, who lays down his life for the sheep, leaving the ninety-nine to go after the one lost sheep. He waited patiently for the sinner at the well, welcomed himself into

Zacchaeus's home, and reached out to touch the untouchable—like the leper—showing mercy and grace in every encounter. He ate with tax collectors and sinners, boldly declaring that he came to seek and save the lost, not the righteous.

Jesus came not to condemn or judge but to heal, to save, and to restore, giving his life as a ransom for many. He himself took away infirmities and bore our diseases. A simple touch from him healed the woman with the twelve-year blood flow, demonstrating the power of faith and grace.

He is Immanuel, God with us, and the great Light shining in the darkness. He did not merely proclaim the kingdom of God; he was the Kingdom of God in person, bringing its life and power wherever he went. Through his life and his words—words that are "spirit and life"—he reveals the fullness of God's love and truth.

He trained his disciples to continue the work he was doing and assured them that even greater works they would do. He called them to deny themselves, to set their hearts on the things of God. He revealed himself as the rest for all who toil and are burdened, declaring himself the LORD of the Sabbath.

He came as the word, and the word became flesh, full of grace and truth. In him was life, and the life was the light of men. He is the Lamb of God who takes away the sin of the world. He taught concerning the need to be born of the Spirit. He revealed himself as the living water, inviting all to come to him and drink. He is the Bread of Life, whose words are spirit and life.

SALT OF THE EARTH AND LIGHT OF THE WORLD

But Jesus was not only the perfect embodiment of God's kingdom; He also taught and proclaimed its nature and values. Through his teachings, he revealed the constitution of the kingdom—the poor in spirit, those who mourn, the meek, the pure in heart, the peacemakers, and those who hunger and thirst for righteousness. He called his followers to be the salt of the earth and the light of the world, illuminating darkness with truth and love.

As a man, Jesus was a carpenter, a craftsman working with ordinary materials, shaping and building with skilled hands. Now, as students of science and seekers of knowledge, you too are called to be salt and light in your world. Just as salt preserves, flavors, and heals, and light exposes, guides, and warms, so you are invited to influence your fields with integrity, wisdom, and compassion.

In your laboratories, classrooms, and future workplaces, how will you embody this calling? How will you let the love, truth, and grace of Christ shape your work, your discoveries, and your relationships? To be salt and light is to reflect Christ's character by living faithfully, speaking truth with kindness, and serving others with humility and courage.

ROOTED IN THE LIVING WORD

College life can feel like a whirlwind, full of intellectual challenges, social pressures, and cultural noise. In the midst of this, being rooted in God's word is essential. Scripture does more than inform us; it renews our mind and transforms our soul. It shapes our identity, purpose, and direction. Like the early pioneers of modern science—Robert Boyle, Isaac Newton, and others—who saw their scientific work as a form of worship, individuals today can draw from Scripture to align their academic pursuits with God's will.

The idea of being made in God's image can sometimes feel distant or abstract. But in Jesus Christ, that image is made clear and real. Paul calls him "the image of the invisible God" (Col 1:15), and Hebrews describes him as "the radiance of God's glory" (Heb 1:3). In Jesus, we see God's wisdom, power, and love fully expressed in a way we can understand. Because of him, we come to know who we truly are and what we were created for. Paul explains that "the knowledge of the glory of God in the face of Jesus Christ" (2 Cor 4:6) is where true wisdom and understanding begin.

Scripture is not simply a collection of sacred writings or a moral compass to follow—it is living truth that reveals a Person. Jesus said, "You search the Scriptures because you think that in them you have eternal life; and it is they that bear witness about Me" (John 5:39). The Bible does not merely point toward wisdom; it points toward Christ, who is Wisdom embodied. To open the Scriptures with a seeking heart is to encounter the One who speaks life, anchors identity, and transforms the soul. Those who build their lives on his words are like wise builders who lay their foundation on the rock (Matt 7:24–25). Such a foundation stands firm—not only in seasons of growth and success, but also in times of trial: through intellectual doubts, cultural pressures, and personal challenges.

Hebrews 4:12 describes the Word of God as "living and active, sharper than any two-edged sword, piercing to the division of soul and spirit . . . and discerning the thoughts and intentions of the heart." Especially for those in scientific disciplines, approaching the Bible as the living word—full of Spirit and life (John 6:63)—means allowing it to shape the whole being, not just worldview or ethics. Immersed in Scripture, one does not merely read facts or rules; but encounters the living Christ who speaks to the heart, transforms the mind, and empowers actions. The word of God is not merely a written text but the living Logos—Jesus Christ Himself—who became flesh (John 1:14). When Scripture is read and heard, it is brought to life by the Holy Spirit, who quickens our spirits and empowers transformation. In this way, the Word, Christ, and the Spirit are inseparably united in the ongoing work of revelation, sanctification, and empowerment (John 6:63)."

FAITH AND THE ACADEMIC JOURNEY

Faith is the engine of the believer's journey, ignited and nurtured by hearing the word of Christ. This enables us to call on his name and receive salvation. The connection between the word and calling on the LORD shows that Scripture is not merely information—it is a living encounter that ignites and sustains our relationship with God (Rom 10:17). In academic environments where skepticism and self-reliance often dominate, faith rooted in Scripture becomes a source of strength and clarity. Paul reminded the Galatians that the Spirit is received not by human effort but by faith through hearing (Gal 3:2). Therefore, believers are urged to "let the word of Christ dwell in you richly" (Col 3:16)—allowing Scripture to shape thoughts, choices, values, and relationships.

Engaging deeply with Scripture nurtures and strengthens faith. The process of faith-building is both intellectual and relational. Through the word, believers come to know God's character, his promises, and his purposes intimately. This knowledge deepens love for God and strengthens the resolve to follow him fully in work, personal life, and future vocation.

But this foundation in Christ is not for personal benefit alone. As lives are transformed by the word, individuals become living witnesses of Christ in classrooms, laboratories, and communities. Paul writes, "Now the LORD is the Spirit, and where the Spirit of the LORD is, there is freedom . . . we all, with unveiled faces, are being transformed into the same image from one degree of glory to another" (2 Cor 3:17–18). The Bible becomes both mirror and map, reflecting who they are in Christ and guiding who they are becoming.

The Bible is God-breathed and "useful for teaching, rebuking, correcting, and training in righteousness" (2 Tim 3:16–17). It equips believers for every good work, including scientific exploration, ethical decision-making, and leadership. Peter exhorts believers to "crave pure spiritual milk, so that by it you may grow up in your salvation" (1 Pet 2:2). Jesus promises that those who remain in him and his word will bear abundant fruit (John 15:7), and that the word planted in hearts, if not choked by worldly distractions, will produce a rich harvest (Matt 13:22).

The word of God is like a seed planted in the soil of our hearts. For the seed to grow strong and bear fruit, the soil, our hearts, must be pure and receptive. When our hearts are open and free from hardness or distraction, the word takes root, grows, and produces a harvest of love, joy, and peace.

Just as newborn babies long for pure, nourishing milk, so we should crave the "guileless milk of the Word" (1 Pet 2:2). This pure spiritual nourishment is essential for growth toward salvation and maturity in Christ. When we "taste that the LORD is good" (1 Pet

2:3), we find the word both satisfying and life-giving, encouraging us to seek it daily. This longing nurtures faith and strengthens our hearts for the challenges of academic life and beyond.

SCRIPTURE: LIVING, ACTIVE, AND TRANSFORMING

The New Testament invites us to ground our identity, pursuits, and aspirations firmly in Christ. Through Scripture, our minds are continually renewed (Rom 12:2), our character is shaped, and we are empowered for our unique calling. Whether in the lab, the lecture hall, or moments of quiet reflection, God's word provides the wisdom, clarity, and strength to live a faithful, fruitful life.

Those who build their lives on this foundation, Christ and his word, will not only thrive in their work and studies but also shine as lights in the world, glorifying God through both knowledge and character. Lives become living testimonies to the power of God's truth, bearing fruit not only in accomplishments but in quiet integrity, humility, and resilient hope. This is the essence of integrating faith and learning: not separating the spiritual from the intellectual, but allowing the Spirit of God to transform every pursuit, scientific inquiry, writing, collaboration, or service, into an offering of worship.

Whether solving complex equations, preparing presentations, or engaging in difficult conversations, every effort becomes sacred, infused with purpose, guided by truth, and shaped by grace. In doing so, we reflect the very nature of Christ, who is wisdom incarnate (1 Cor 1:24), and our lives glorify God in every dimension.

Just as the Israelites gathered manna each morning in the wilderness (Exod 16:21), we are called to seek God daily through his word and prayer. Manna could not be stored for the next day; it had to be collected fresh each morning before the sun grew hot. In the same way, our spiritual nourishment cannot be stockpiled but must be received daily, directly from God. Jesus reminds us, "The words that I have spoken to you are spirit and are life" (John

6:63). His words are not mere teachings; they are living substance. They quicken our spirit, infuse our soul with clarity and peace, and guide us with divine breath. Like manna in the wilderness, they are daily bread, nourishing us with life that cannot be found elsewhere. (John 6:32–35), invites us to begin each day in communion with him, drawing life and direction from his presence. In feeding on Christ daily, we deepen our roots in him, drawing nourishment that sustains us through every challenge.

Setting aside time in the early morning to meet with the LORD, before the noise and demands of the day take over, is a habit that builds spiritual resilience and sharpens focus. Just as physical food sustains the body, so too does the Word of God feed the soul. Those who prioritize this time find that their minds are renewed, their burdens lifted, and their decisions aligned with God's wisdom. The secret strength of many faithful believers, past and present, has been this hidden manna: the quiet, early-morning encounters with God that anchor the day and cultivate intimacy with him.

The result of this ongoing, reflective engagement is transformation. Just as grass is miraculously turned into milk—something nourishing, life-giving, and sustaining—so the Word of God, when digested deeply, becomes wisdom, peace, and strength within us. It begins to nourish others through our speech, our decisions, and our presence. Scripture that is merely heard may be forgotten, but Scripture that is meditated on becomes part of us—forming character, guiding choices, and bearing fruit in our lives.

God's word, when gathered and treasured in the heart over time, becomes like honey: "sweeter than honey, even honey from the comb" (Ps 19:10). Just as bees transform pollen into something nourishing and long-lasting, so the Spirit transforms our daily engagement with Scripture into inner strength, Christlike character, and the ability to speak with grace and truth.

SPIRITUAL NOURISHMENT: DAILY MANNA

Those who consistently draw near to God, gathering his Word like manna each morning, meditating on it like cows chewing the cud, and patiently collecting truth like bees gathering nectar, become like trees transplanted beside streams of living water. Their roots grow deep into the soil of God's Word, drawing strength, nourishment, and stability. As Isaiah says, they will "take root downward and bear fruit upward" (Isa 37:31). The Psalmist echoes this: "They are like a tree planted by streams of water, which yields its fruit in season and whose leaf does not wither, whatever they do prospers" (Ps 1:3).

In a world of shifting values and pressures, these rooted lives stand firm. They flourish, not by rushing or striving, but by abiding. And in their flourishing, they bless others, offering the fruit of wisdom, peace, and godly influence wherever they are planted.

BUILDING ON THE ROCK: THE FOUNDATION OF CHRIST

In Matthew 7:24-27, Jesus tells the story of two men—one wise, one foolish. Both built houses, but only one chose the right foundation. The wise man built his house on a rock, and when the rain fell and the floods came, it stood firm. The foolish man built on sand. When the storm came, his house fell with a great crash.

This parable isn't just about buildings—it's about lives. Jesus said the difference between these two builders lies in this: "Everyone who hears these words of Mine and puts them into practice is like a wise man . . . " (Matt 7:24).

To build on the rock is to listen carefully to God's word, take it to heart, and live by it. It means letting Scripture shape how we think, how we relate to others, how we make decisions, and how we respond to trials.

This is especially important. The university years are a time of construction, of building habits, character, convictions, and a future. Will these be built on the shifting sands of popular opinion, personal ambition, or cultural pressure? Or will they be grounded in the unchanging truth of God's Word?

Storms of stress, disappointment, and doubt will come. But if your foundation is Scripture, read, trusted, and obeyed, you will not fall. You will stand firm, because your life is built on the Rock.

These formative years are like the laying of a foundation and the framing of a house—each thought a brick, each decision a beam. Will the structure rise on the shifting sands of opinion, ambition, and cultural noise? Or will it be anchored in the unshakable bedrock of God's word? Scripture calls us to "let the word of Christ dwell in you richly" (Col 3:16), not merely as a guest, but as a permanent resident shaping every room of our inner life. When his Word fills the halls of our hearts, wisdom becomes the architecture, peace the paint on the walls, and gratitude the light pouring through the windows. A life built this way does not sway with the storm; it stands, beautiful and enduring, a dwelling fit for the presence of God.

ACTIVITY 1 : CHRIST IN ALL: A PERIODIC TABLE REFLECTION FROM COLOSSIANS

This activity is developed based on the book of Colossians, though any book of the Bible or topic can be selected. The author herself used the topic of "glory" in the classroom. In this activity, students will engage throughout the semester with selected verses from Colossians, each highlighting a unique aspect of Christ's person and work. From these passages, they will extract key phrases or truths and record them in individual boxes on a blank periodic table template. By the end of the term, the completed table will serve as a visual and conceptual portrait of the Christ revealed in Colossians.

For example: *The Son is the image of the invisible God* (1:15), *the firstborn over all creation* (1:15), *for in him all things were created* (1:16), *all things have been created through him and for him* (1:16b), *he is before all things* (1:17a), *in him all things hold together*

(1:17b), *he is the head of the body, the church* (1:18), *the beginning and the firstborn from among the dead* (1:18), *so that in everything he might have the supremacy* (1:18), *for God was pleased to have all his fullness dwell in him* (1:19), and *through him to reconcile to himself all things . . . by making peace through his blood, shed on the cross* (1:20).

Students may also write a brief reflective paragraph on their "Christ-centered periodic table," explaining how this integrative process has deepened their understanding of Christ and drawn their heart to love him.

ACTIVITY 2: SALT OF THE EARTH AND LIGHT OF THE WORLD

God is light, Christ is light, and the opening of God's word gives light. This can be demonstrated through a simple experiment. Pure water doesn't conduct electricity because it lacks free ions. Adding salt dissolves it into ions, transforming the water to conduct electricity. In the same way, when we immerse ourselves in God's word and Spirit, invisible changes within us transform how we "conduct" ourselves in the world. This illustrates how, just as pure water is transformed by the addition of salt, we too are transformed when we allow our hearts to turn to God and immerse ourselves in his Word.

Materials

- 1 small beaker or cup of pure water
- Table salt (NaCl)
- Simple electrical circuit setup (e.g., battery, wires, small light bulb or LED)
- Stirring rod or spoon

Procedure

1. Set up the circuit: Connect the battery, wires, and light bulb so that the bulb will light if the water conducts electricity (this set-up you can buy).
2. Test pure water: Pour pure water into the container and complete the circuit. Observe that the bulb does not light, illustrating that pure water does not conduct electricity.
3. Add salt: Dissolve a small amount of table salt into the water. Stir until fully dissolved.
4. Test salt water: Place the electrodes into the salt water and complete the circuit. Observe that the bulb now lights, showing that the water conducts electricity after salt is added.

Reflection Questions

- How does Jesus' example of living fully submitted to the Father's will challenge or inspire the way you approach your academic and personal life?
- In what ways does building your life on the "rock" of Scripture provide stability during times of academic pressure, doubt, or uncertainty?
- How has creating your "Christ-centered periodic table" helped you see connections between your faith and your study of science?
- As "salt and light" in your future field, how do you envision embodying Christ's character—integrity, compassion, wisdom—in practical ways within your academic or professional journey?

9

Chemistry
The Central Science Revealing Divine Design

FROM THE VASTNESS OF galaxies to the steady rhythm of a heartbeat, the universe operates through the processes of chemistry. The air we breathe and the way a leaf turns toward the sun are made possible by chemical interactions that are both orderly and precise. Occurring on scales from the microscopic to the cosmic, these processes underscore the central role of chemistry in sustaining life and shaping the natural world. Far from being merely a branch of science, chemistry provides the fundamental structures and principles through which the natural world is organized and understood, from the arrangement of atoms to the interactions of molecules.

As we examine the principles that govern bonding and reactions, we begin to see more than mechanisms; we perceive intention. The Apostle Paul reminds us that "in him all things hold together" (Col 1:17), and chemistry reflects this truth: a cosmos maintained by precise forces, calibrated energies, and patterns so reliable that they sustain galaxies and guide enzymes alike.

Yet chemistry is not merely functional; it is formative. Water does more than hydrate; it nurtures. Carbon does more than bond; it builds. From the calcium in coral reefs to the nitrogen in our neurons, chemistry reveals a universe that is both interconnected and purposeful. Its laws demonstrate consistency, and its structures display design.

This faithful precision is evident not only in distant galaxies but also in the everyday. Consider a simple glass of milk: calcium, essential for bones and teeth, is largely insoluble on its own. Yet in milk, it becomes bioavailable through chelation to specific amino acids in casein, a milk protein. Through this molecular arrangement, calcium remains suspended and soluble in water-based systems, enabling nourishment for the young of mammals. From the grass that cows consume to the milk they produce, chemistry orchestrates a quiet but life-giving transformation.

This is not merely biochemistry; it is a metaphor for grace. Peter exhorts believers to "long for the pure spiritual milk of the word" (1 Pet 2:2), suggesting that just as newborns require milk for growth, our souls require the sustenance of truth. Ordinary milk becomes extraordinary, reflecting divine providence where molecular design mirrors spiritual nourishment.

Even the simplest chemical reaction illustrates this truth: molecules must collide with sufficient energy of activation to overcome the barrier for the reaction to proceed. Spiritually, this reminds us that those who receive God's abundant provision of grace will reign in life through Jesus Christ. Just as molecules require the right energy to transform, we depend on Christ, relying on his life and resurrection power rather than our own effort. Grace is not "I" but Christ, and apart from him we can do nothing.

Consider, too, the principle of chemical equilibrium, where reactions occur simultaneously in forward and reverse directions until their rates balance. At this dynamic point, concentrations of reactants and products may appear stable, yet transformation continues at the molecular level. This quiet persistence mirrors spiritual life: as 2 Corinthians 3:18 declares, "And we all, who with unveiled faces contemplate the LORD's glory, are being transformed into his image with ever-increasing glory, which comes from the LORD, who is the Spirit." Nature offers a striking illustration: stalactites and stalagmites form drop by drop as calcium carbonate slowly precipitates over time, creating intricate cave formations without haste. As in chemical equilibrium, lasting strength and beauty emerge through patient and faithful processes, sustained by grace, refined through endurance, and unfolding in hope rather than through sudden or superficial change.

To study chemistry, then, is not simply to learn; it is to behold. It is to trace the fingerprints of God in the smallest particles and the largest systems, to worship through observation, and to respond with stewardship, humility, and awe.

THE PERIODIC TABLE AND ELEMENTS: BLUEPRINT AND BUILDING BLOCKS OF CREATION

The periodic table is one of science's most iconic tools. At first glance, it appears as a grid of symbols and numbers. Look closer, and it reveals a profound map of the universe's fundamental building blocks. Each element's placement and the patterns within the table reflect deep order and intentionality, inviting both wonder and reflection. For those with eyes of faith, the periodic table is more than a chart; it is a blueprint of creation itself.

Organized by atomic number, the count of protons in each nucleus, the table arranges elements with similar chemical properties into groups or families. This structure mirrors how electron arrangements govern atomic behavior. Group 1 elements, the alkali metals, are highly reactive, while Group 18 elements, the noble gases, are remarkably stable. Patterns such as atomic radius, ionization energy, and reactivity reveal an elegant logic woven into the universe, pointing to the wisdom behind creation.

Although there are just over 100 known elements, they combine in countless ways to form mountains, oceans, plants, animals, and the technologies that shape our world. Carbon forms the backbone of life; oxygen fuels respiration; iron carries oxygen in blood; silicon builds computer chips. Sodium bonds with chlorine to create table salt, giving water its taste and supporting life itself. Water sustains every cell, while trees and plants, composed of these elements, produce compounds that heal and nourish, forming the basis of medicines. The periodic table does more than list elements; it organizes the principles governing their interactions, providing a key to understanding the complexity and beauty of creation.

From a spiritual perspective, this design echoes Psalm 104:24: "How many are your works, LORD! In wisdom you made them all; the earth is full of your creatures." Each element contributes to creation's harmony, enabling not only life but the experience of life itself—taste, touch, and healing. Elements were made to relate, bond, and build, reflecting the relational and purposeful nature of God's creation.

Humans were formed "from the dust of the ground" (Gen 2:7), dust that is chemical in nature, composed of the very elements that make soil and stars. God breathed life into this dust, endowing it with spirit and meaning, giving us a dual identity: physical and spiritual, elemental and eternal. How we steward these elements matters profoundly. Misusing them distorts their purpose, but caring for them joins us in God's ongoing work of creation.

CARBON: THE BACKBONE OF LIFE

Within this elemental framework, carbon stands out for its versatility and centrality to life. Its ability to form four stable covalent bonds enables chains, rings, branches, and complex three-dimensional structures—the foundation of all living systems. Carbohydrates store energy; proteins perform cellular functions; lipids form membranes and reserves; nucleic acids carry genetic instructions. Every fold, twist, and interaction in cells depends on carbon's ability to unite atoms into meaningful structures.

Carbon balances stability with flexibility. Its bonds are strong enough to maintain life's intricate molecules yet flexible enough to allow continual transformation. This tension mirrors life itself: growth, adaptation, and renewal. At the heart of identity lies carbon's role in DNA, whose carbon-based backbone carries instructions defining every organism.

Carbon's influence extends through a vast, interconnected cycle linking atmosphere, organisms, oceans, and fossil fuels. Plants capture carbon dioxide through photosynthesis, converting it into organic compounds. Animals incorporate carbon into tissues and release it back as carbon dioxide through respiration. Death returns carbon to the soil, and over millions of years it can become fossil fuels or, under extreme pressure, diamonds. In oceans, carbon forms calcium carbonate structures like coral reefs and shells, sustaining ecosystems and storing carbon long-term.

This cycle reflects profound spiritual truths. Carbon moves through life, death, and renewal, echoing creation's rhythms and God's redemptive work. The elements composing our bodies and the earth carry meaning beyond material form, testifying to a Creator who is both artist and sustainer. To know carbon is to glimpse wisdom woven into life's fabric, calling us to reverence and stewardship. Each breath of carbon dioxide we exhale participates in this sacred cycle of connection, purpose, and transformation.

The periodic table and its elements are more than data. They are gifts entrusted to us as caretakers of creation. Recognizing the divine intentionality etched into every atom allows us to glimpse the heart of God—the master craftsman whose precision, creativity, and care sustain all things.

CHEMISTRY'S CREATIVE POWER

From ancient dyes extracted from insects to lifesaving modern medicines, chemistry has always been a force of transformation. It shapes the world around us, from the energy that powers our homes to the food that nourishes our bodies. With such potential comes responsibility. When rightly practiced, chemistry becomes more than innovation; it participates in God's ongoing creative work.

In medicine, chemistry reveals the molecular foundations of health. Drugs combat infections, regulate neurological conditions, and target cancer cells with precision. Advances in medicinal chemistry have led to more effective cancer therapies, including treatments that attack malignant cells while sparing healthy tissue. Discoveries such as antibiotics and anesthetics have saved countless lives, demonstrating chemistry's profound impact on human well-being.

In energy, chemistry enables storage, conversion, and efficient use of power. From fossil fuels to biofuels and lithium-ion batteries to hydrogen cells, chemistry designs the materials and reactions that light homes and move vehicles.

In agriculture, chemistry nourishes the world. Fertilizers increase yields, pesticides protect harvests, and preservation techniques extend shelf life. These chemical innovations underpin global food security.

In materials science, chemistry transforms elements into the tools of daily life: alloys for airplanes, polymers for medical devices, semiconductors for computers, and plastics for countless applications. Chemistry makes the invisible visible, shaping the fabric of human life.

Even the smallest particle reveals the grandeur of creation. Within every atom lies a nucleus, bound by forces of unimaginable strength, holding protons and neutrons together with a precision that sustains matter itself. When a chemist probes this realm, it becomes clear that the structure of the universe is not random. The stability of atoms, the balance of nuclear forces, and the profound relationship between mass and energy, captured in Einstein's $E = mc^2$, all point to a deep and sustaining order.

For those who explore this microscopic world, it is difficult to see it as merely material. At the heart of every atom, one can sense the invisible hand of the Creator—the same Christ in whom "all things hold together" (Col 1:17). To study the nucleus is to glimpse the sustaining power of God, a reminder that the laws of physics and chemistry reflect the wisdom, precision, and care of the One who crafted the cosmos. Even in the atom's smallest spaces, chemistry points to something eternal. Every reaction, every bond, and every particle is evidence of a reality that transcends human understanding. For the chemist, the pursuit of knowledge becomes a form of worship, a journey into the depths of matter that leads to awe and reverence for the Creator.

In each of these realms, chemistry is a channel of creativity, shaping, healing, solving, and sustaining. With such power comes a deeper responsibility: to act with wisdom, integrity, and respect for the Creator's design.

We trust in the power of chemistry even when we cannot see the reactions themselves. Our confidence comes from observing the outcomes, experiencing their effects, and recognizing their consistency. Similarly, a common person cannot know the detailed workings that make medicine effective, yet we trust it works.

Faith mirrors this trust. Just as chemical processes are invisible yet real, Christ works within us even when unseen. Science trains the mind to recognize patterns and cause-and-effect; faith trains the heart to perceive God's sustaining presence. Both invite trust in realities that cannot always be directly observed.

ACTIVITY: THE UNSEEN YET REAL PRESENCE OF CHRIST — THE BLUE BOTTLE EXPERIMENT

In this experiment, an alkaline glucose solution reduces methylene blue from blue to colorless. Shaking the solution dissolves oxygen, re-oxidizing the dye, and the cycle repeats. The color changes provide a visible sign of invisible reactions at work.

This experiment illustrates faith: Christ is present and active in our lives even when we cannot see him. Just as we trust chemical processes to produce predictable results, we trust in God's promises and sustaining power. Faith is not blind; it is grounded in truth, experience, and God's Word. As Scripture reminds us:

> "The LORD be with your spirit." — 2 Timothy 4:22
>
> "I am with you always, to the very end of the age." — Matthew 28:20
>
> "Though you have not seen him, you love him . . . you are filled with inexpressible and glorious joy." — 1 Peter 1:8-9

Materials

- Eye protection (goggles)
- 1 dm³ conical flask
- Stopper or bung to seal the flask
- Potassium hydroxide (KOH), 8 g (corrosive, irritant)
- Glucose (dextrose), 10 g
- Methylene blue, 0.05 g (harmful)
- Ethanol (Industrial Denatured Alcohol), 50 cm³ (highly flammable, harmful)

Preparation

1. Prepare a methylene blue solution by dissolving 0.05 g of methylene blue in 50 mL of ethanol (0.1% solution).
2. Weigh 8 g of potassium hydroxide into the conical flask.
3. Add 300 mL of water and 10 g of glucose to the flask. Swirl gently until solids are fully dissolved.
4. Add 5 mL of the methylene blue solution to the flask (exact amount is not critical).
5. The solution will initially appear blue but should turn colorless after about one minute.
6. Stopper the flask.
7. Hold the stopper securely and shake the flask vigorously to introduce oxygen into the solution.
8. The solution will turn blue as methylene blue is oxidized by the dissolved oxygen.
9. The blue color will gradually fade back to colorless over approximately 30 seconds as the glucose reduces the methylene blue.

10. Repeated shaking will reintroduce oxygen, and the cycle of blue to colorless can be observed multiple times—over 20 cycles are possible.
11. Note that the more vigorously the solution is shaken, the longer the blue color persists before fading.
12. After several hours, the solution may turn yellow and the color changes will no longer occur.

Safety Notes

- Always wear eye protection when preparing and handling chemicals.
- Potassium hydroxide is corrosive and irritating; handle with care.
- Methylene blue is harmful if ingested or inhaled; avoid direct contact.
- Ethanol is highly flammable; keep away from open flames and heat sources.
- Dispose of the solution according to local safety regulations.

Reflection Questions

- How does the structure and order of the periodic table reflect both scientific principles and a sense of divine intentionality?
- In what ways does carbon's unique bonding ability illustrate the balance between stability and flexibility in life, and how might this mirror spiritual truths about growth and renewal?
- How can understanding the chemical processes in everyday substances like milk and honey deepen our appreciation of God's provision and grace?

Chemistry, Faith, and Stewardship

- What ethical responsibilities do we have as stewards of chemistry and the elements, especially considering the impact of chemical use on communities and the environment?
- The Blue Bottle experiment illustrates trusting in unseen realities. How does this scientific analogy deepen your faith in Christ's unseen but active presence in your life?

10

Stewardship in Chemistry
Guiding the Next Generation of Innovators

IF WE HAVE SEEN chemistry as a window into God's wisdom, revealing the unseen forces that sustain creation, then we are called to respond. Chemistry is not only a lens to observe transformation; it is a responsibility. The chemist's calling is twofold to understand these transformations and to participate in them with integrity, care, and purpose. Every reaction, every element, and every molecule carries potential—both to harm and to heal. Stewardship begins when we see the earth not as raw material for human use but as a sacred gift entrusted to our care. Science becomes a vocation when it serves others and honors the Creator.

As we reflect on the molecular precision and order of creation, it becomes clear that chemists are called to act with foresight, humility, and moral responsibility. Knowledge and skill alone are not enough; they must be guided by ethical insight and love for creation. In the laboratory and beyond, every decision regarding materials, processes, or applications sends ripples into ecosystems, communities, and future generations.

Through this perspective, stewardship emerges naturally. Green chemistry, systems thinking, life cycle assessment, and ethical design become more than technical practices; they are expressions of care, responsibility, and faith. Understanding the impact of chemicals on people and the environment is an act of reverence and a tangible way to participate in God's sustaining work in the world.

SYSTEMS THINKING AND STEWARDSHIP IN CHEMISTRY

The 2023 World Economic Forum[1] highlights systems thinking[2] as a core skill for the future workforce. As industries increasingly embrace sustainable practices, there is a growing demand for graduates who can think holistically, understanding not only chemical reactions but also the broader social, environmental, and ethical implications of those reactions. The pressing challenges of our time; climate instability, pollution, resource scarcity, and health inequities, demand more than technical innovation; they require moral courage and vision.

Green chemistry,[3] systems thinking, and life cycle assessment[4] are more than technical tools, they embody ethical responsibility. Chemistry that minimizes waste, avoids hazardous substances, and advances sustainability aligns with the biblical call to care for creation and love our neighbors. In this light, the chemist becomes a steward, one who practices science with reverence, restraint, and hope.

Higher education plays a vital role in forming this next generation of chemists. Within its halls, students are shaped not only by knowledge but by virtue. Laboratory safety echoes the call to care for life; environmental consciousness reflects the biblical call to justice and mercy. Students trained in such an environment

---

1. World Economic Forum, *Annual Report 2023–2024*.
2. Tümay, *Systems Thinking in Chemistry and Chemical Education*, 3927.
3. Anastas and Warner, *Green Chemistry*, 25.
4. Matthews, Hendrickson, and Matthews, *Life Cycle Assessment*, 42.

are not merely future researchers or industry professionals, they are potential healers, reformers, and faithful stewards of creation.

This vision is not naive optimism but a bold call to action. The world needs chemists who dare to see science as a sacred trust, who will ask hard questions about the materials they use, the impact they leave, and the systems they participate in. Chemists who will bring compassion into laboratories, justice into supply chains, and humility into discovery. Such a life will not be easy.

Through this formation, the next generation is equipped not only to innovate but to embody a renewed vision for chemistry, one rooted in worship, service, and redemption.

CHEMISTRY AT A CROSSROADS

The 21st century presents profound challenges. Climate change accelerates, ecosystems falter, and human health faces new and emerging threats. Chemistry stands at a crossroads: it can either continue contributing to these global problems or rise to lead in solving them. Many chemicals and processes today carry unintended consequences. Industrial emissions have contaminated air and water; persistent toxins have disrupted delicate ecosystems; and continued dependence on fossil fuels threatens the stability of the planet's climate.

Historical lessons illuminate this urgency. The widespread use of DDT, once celebrated as a miracle pesticide, caused ecological disruption and human health impacts due to its persistence and bioaccumulation. The Bhopal disaster of 1984, where methyl isocyanate gas leaked from a pesticide plant, led to thousands of deaths and long-term suffering. Mercury contamination in Minamata, Japan, and oil spills such as the Exxon Valdez release of 1989 devastated marine ecosystems and local communities. Persistent organic pollutants (POPs) regulated under the Stockholm Convention (2001) continue to accumulate in humans and wildlife, exemplifying the lasting harm of chemical mismanagement.

These events underscore the need for a fundamental transformation: moving from chemistry as invention toward chemistry as intentional and responsible stewardship. Educators and practitioners must embrace systems thinking and life cycle assessment, designing all chemical products and processes to minimize harm. Global frameworks, including the United Nations Sustainable Development Goals (SDGs), provide guidance for aligning chemical practice with justice, sustainability, and human flourishing.

CHEMISTRY AND THE UNITED NATIONS SUSTAINABLE DEVELOPMENT GOALS (UN SDGS)

Chemistry plays a pivotal role in achieving the 17 SDGs, which call for urgent action to end poverty, improve health and education, reduce inequality, and combat climate change while preserving ecosystems. Green and sustainable chemistry directly supports this global agenda.

- Designing safer chemicals aligns with SDG 3 (Good Health and Well-being) and SDG 6 (Clean Water and Sanitation) by reducing exposure to toxins.

- Use of renewable feedstocks and design for degradation support SDG 12 (Responsible Consumption and Production) and SDG 13 (Climate Action).

- Energy efficiency and waste prevention contribute to SDG 7 (Affordable and Clean Energy) and SDG 11 (Sustainable Cities and Communities).

When students connect chemical practices with global consequences, chemistry is revealed not only as a subject but as a tool for addressing real-world challenges. Educating future chemists with the SDGs in mind nurtures a generation that designs with purpose—aware that molecules and materials shape human and planetary well-being.

STEWARDSHIP IN CHEMISTRY

DEFINING STEWARDSHIP FOR CHEMISTS

Stewardship embodies care, foresight, and profound responsibility. Every action, whether in the laboratory, industry, or policy, sends ripples through time, influencing ecosystems, communities, and future generations. To be a steward is to manage knowledge, tools, and creative capacities with humility, wisdom, and vision.

Stewardship calls for reimagining how chemicals are conceived, developed, utilized, and disposed of. It requires moving beyond short-term utility, cost, or efficiency to embrace a broader perspective, weighing long-term consequences on human health, ecosystems, and societal well-being. Ethical questions arise: not only "Can this be done?" but also "Should this be done?" Stewardship demands that innovations support life, sustainability, and values that transcend immediate gains.

GREEN CHEMISTRY: A PATHWAY FORWARD

Green chemistry offers a clear and actionable framework rooted in both scientific rigor and ethical responsibility. Grounded in its 12 Principles, green chemistry guides chemists to innovate with intention, designing processes and products that honor creation rather than exploit it. These principles encourage chemists to:

1. Prevent waste rather than treat or clean it up afterward, recognizing that prevention is better than cure not only for human health but for the earth itself.

2. Use renewable feedstocks and materials, reflecting a trust in the ongoing cycles of nature that God has established.

3. Minimize energy consumption, honoring the gift of creation by avoiding unnecessary depletion of resources.

4. Design safer chemicals and products that degrade harmlessly in the environment, embodying a commitment to protect life and promote restoration.

Systems thinking and life cycle assessment expand focus beyond individual reactions, considering full environmental and societal impacts. Chemistry and toxicology are intertwined: chemists understand molecular behavior, while toxicologists evaluate health effects, enabling proactive reduction of harm.

STEWARDSHIP IN ACTION: CONTEMPORARY CHALLENGES AND INITIATIVES

The first Stockholm Declaration on Chemistry[5] for the Future underscored the urgent need for chemistry to serve justice and sustainability. It called for chemists to act as stewards, guiding innovation in ways that benefit technological progress while promoting the flourishing of people and the planet. Stewardship sharpens creativity by framing scientific work within the context of environmental care, community well-being, and ethical responsibility.

Current research highlights how critical this approach is. Persistent chemicals such as per- and polyfluoroalkyl substances (PFAS), widely used in industrial and consumer products, demonstrate the long-term consequences of chemical design choices. PFAS are highly persistent in the environment, accumulate in living systems, and are linked to adverse health effects, illustrating the need for proactive design, hazard assessment, and ethical consideration in chemical innovation. Other historical and contemporary cases—such as pesticide overuse, chemical spills, industrial leaks, and oil disasters—provide sobering examples of how chemistry, when practiced without stewardship, can harm ecosystems and communities for decades.

Beyond academia, numerous organizations and initiatives reinforce this vision of stewardship. The American Chemical Society (ACS), through its Green Chemistry Institute, supports education, research, and professional development aimed at

5. Stockholm Declaration on Chemistry for the Future.

safer, sustainable chemical practices. Beyond Benign, a nonprofit, develops laboratory curricula and community programs to make green chemistry accessible and actionable. Collaborative efforts in the pharmaceutical and chemical industries—including round tables and sustainability forums—encourage the adoption of green synthesis, waste reduction, energy efficiency, and renewable feedstocks, demonstrating that responsible chemistry can coexist with innovation and economic success.

GREENING UNDERGRADUATE CHEMISTRY LABORATORIES

As the chemical enterprise increasingly embraces sustainability, undergraduate education plays a crucial role in forming the next generation of chemists. Laboratory experiences are often the most formative and memorable aspect of a chemistry education, yet traditional labs have historically emphasized technique and yield over environmental and ethical responsibility. Slowly, academia is responding: institutions and educators are embedding the 12 Principles of Green Chemistry into hands-on experiments, fostering systems thinking, sustainability awareness, and ethical reasoning.

Redesigned laboratories[6] can transform student learning while promoting stewardship. Labs must be designed with the 12 Principles of Green Chemistry in mind to fully support the United Nations Sustainable Development Goals (UN SDGs).[7] By using safer, renewable, and environmentally friendly reagents[8], students learn to consider the full life cycle of chemical products—from raw material sourcing to disposal. Such approaches encourage reflection on human health and ecological impacts, cultivate ethical reasoning, and foster a mindset that integrates scientific skill with

---

6. Abraham, "A Green Nucleophilic Aromatic Substitution Reaction," 3810-15.
7. Wang, McLenahan, and Abraham, "Using Soapnut Extract."
8. Abraham, Stachow, and Chao, "Cinnamon Oil," 3797-3805.

environmental responsibility.[9] Green chemistry laboratories thus not only teach technical techniques but also nurture a broader vision of chemistry as a practice of stewardship, sustainability, and conscientious innovation.[10]

A VISION FOR FUTURE CHEMISTS

Future chemists are called to steward knowledge wisely, love creation deeply, and act with humility. Chemistry must become a force for justice, healing, and restoration. Whether designing biodegradable materials, replacing hazardous solvents, or challenging unsustainable consumer habits, chemists have the power to shape a better world.

This power must be guided by humility and care. Chemists who honor life and heed creation's groaning produce work that blesses rather than burdens. Educators and students are called to explore creation while guarding it—mending what is broken, redeeming what is misused, and glorifying the Creator in every discovery.

ACTIVITY: STEWARDSHIP-ORIENTED EVALUATION OF EVERYDAY CHEMICAL PRODUCTS

This exercise provides a practical application of stewardship principles. Students are invited to analyze everyday chemical products—such as detergents or personal care items—through the lenses of green chemistry, toxicology, and sustainability. The activity engages them in examining chemical ingredients and their functions, assessing potential human health and environmental hazards, applying life cycle thinking to the product's production,

---

9. Abraham, VanderZwaag, and Chao, "Motivating and Supporting Undergraduate Research," 824-832.

10. Ritter and Abraham, "A Green and Efficient Cyclization," 4134-42.

use, and disposal, and proposing safer, more sustainable alternatives guided by ethical and environmental considerations.

Through this activity, students apply the 12 Principles of Green Chemistry in a tangible context, gaining insight into the interconnected impacts of chemical products on ecosystems and human health. They are encouraged to develop critical thinking and ethical reasoning in chemical design, while reflecting on the chemist's broader responsibility as a steward of creation. The exercise integrates scientific understanding with moral and environmental considerations, fostering a holistic view of chemistry as a vocation that serves both people and the planet.

Procedure

1. Identify all chemical components in the product and categorize their function.
2. Research toxicity, persistence, and bioaccumulation of each ingredient.
3. Evaluate the life cycle from raw material extraction to disposal.
4. Identify opportunities for reducing environmental and human health risks.
5. Suggest modifications or alternatives consistent with green chemistry principles.

Reflection Questions

- How does viewing chemistry as a form of stewardship change the way you think about the role of chemists in society and the environment?
- Reflecting on historical chemical disasters (e.g., Bhopal, Minamata, Exxon Valdez) and persistent pollutants like PFAS, what ethical responsibilities do chemists have in designing and using chemicals today?

- How can the 12 Principles of Green Chemistry and systems thinking guide decision-making in both laboratory and industrial contexts? Provide examples from everyday products or processes.

- In what ways can undergraduate chemistry education be transformed to cultivate environmental consciousness, ethical reasoning, and sustainable innovation in future chemists?

- Considering the United Nations Sustainable Development Goals (SDGs), how can chemists integrate their knowledge and skills to advance human flourishing and ecological sustainability simultaneously?

11

The Spiritual Man
Living with the Mind of Christ

FROM THE BEGINNING GOD'S purpose has been to dwell with humanity. In Genesis, we see him walking with Adam and Eve in the garden. In the Gospels, we see him taking on flesh in the person of Jesus Christ—Immanuel, God with us. In the Epistles, we see the next great step: God not merely with us, but *in us* by his Spirit. And in the final vision of Revelation, heaven and earth are renewed, and God and man are fully one in life, nature, and fellowship. This is not just the story of the Bible; it is the story of us. We are in the renewing process even now. Old things are passing away; all things are becoming new (2 Cor 5:17). The heavens and the earth will be renewed, and so will we.

A RICH LEGACY THAT IS NORMAL FOR THE BELIEVER

Paul wrote to the Corinthians,

> "The person with the Spirit makes judgments about all things, but such a person is not subject to merely human judgments, for, 'Who has known the mind of the LORD

so as to instruct him?' But we have the mind of Christ." (1 Cor 2:15–16)

To "have the mind of Christ" is not a special privilege for a few; it is the normal Christian life. It is the legacy we inherit when Christ lives in us. The spiritual man is one who lives not merely by intellect or emotion, but by the regenerated spirit, in fellowship with God's Spirit.

LIVING BY THE SPIRIT

The spiritual man does not merely *believe* in Christ, he abides in Christ, and Christ abides in him (John 15:4). This abiding changes how we think, how we speak, and how we work. It transforms how we view the world, science, education, and our daily decisions. The mind of Christ sees beyond appearances; it discerns the heart of a matter.

In the laboratory, in the classroom, in the quiet moments of prayer, the spiritual man is not operating from human wisdom alone but from divine insight. Just as the prophets saw visions and the apostles received revelation, the believer today can discern God's leading in every sphere of life.

THE END GOAL: ONENESS

The Bible begins with God creating man in his image and ends with God and man sharing one life and nature. This is the final fulfillment of God's purpose: not simply to have people who worship him from a distance, but to have a corporate people who are his dwelling place, expressing his life in all that they are and do.

OUR INHERITANCE: SCIENTISTS WHO GLORIFIED GOD

From the beginning of this book, we have seen how the wonders of creation, from the smallest atom to the vastness of the cosmos,

THE SPIRITUAL MAN

reflect the hand and heart of God. Science always points to God and draws us closer to him. At its best, it is more than discovery; it is a journey of awe and wonder. Every finding can lead us beyond the material world to the mind of the Creator, turning curiosity into insight and experimentation into a deeper understanding of his design. In this final chapter, we meet the faithful scientists who have gone before us, those who pursued knowledge with brilliance and humility, always seeking to glorify the Creator. Their stories are not just history; they are an inheritance, a rich legacy calling us to join in the adventure.

SANCTIFIED CURIOSITY

God never asked us to abandon our minds. He renews them. The lives of these scientists show that an intellect united with the Spirit can illuminate truth, influence the world, and reflect the Creator's glory. It doesn't idolize science, but honors the Creator through science. And this inheritance calls us not merely to learn, but to discern, to see the deeper truths of God embedded in the created world.

Let us now look closely at three scientists—past and present—whose lives show us what this looks like.

Robert Boyle-Father of Modern Chemistry

One of the most compelling historical examples of a scientist with a renewed mind is Robert Boyle, often called the "father of modern chemistry."[1] As a young man, Boyle experienced a profound encounter with God that shaped his entire life. He vowed to live piously, practicing disciplined daily Bible reading, memorizing Scripture, and studying passages deeply. His devotion extended to academic rigor: he studied Hebrew and Greek, engaged with Jewish scholars such as Menasseh ben Israel, and consulted theologians including James Ussher. Boyle wrote extensively on

---

1. Hunter, *Boyle: Between God and Science*

theology, producing roughly a million words, yet generally avoided controversial doctrinal disputes, focusing instead on personal understanding and devotion.

Boyle distinguished between two forms of divine revelation: Scripture and nature, believing they could not contradict each other. He applied the principle of accommodation, recognizing that the Bible often conveys spiritual truths in accessible language rather than scientific facts. He accepted biblical miracles as authentic events but maintained methodological naturalism in his scientific work, keeping miracles separate from the investigation of nature. Central to his theology was God's sovereignty, freedom, and providence, consistent with the view that God could act beyond natural laws.

Far from being separate from his faith, Boyle's Christian beliefs motivated his scientific endeavors. He sought to extend human dominion over creation responsibly, improve medicine, make it accessible to the poor, and conduct experiments that revealed the Creator's wisdom and goodness. He often likened the universe to a finely constructed clock or machine, whose proper function depended on the skill of its Maker. He insisted that God actively preserves and guides the universe; without divine oversight, the cosmos would collapse. Scientific laws, he argued, are contingent on God's will rather than inherent in matter, so humans must observe the world empirically rather than assume necessity from abstract reasoning.

Boyle's life exemplified the inseparability of science and service. He personally delivered medicines to the sick, including epileptics, and shared pharmaceutical knowledge for charitable use in England and New England, often dedicating up to a third of his income to these efforts. His approach reflected faith-driven philanthropy and intellectual humility, acknowledging human limitations while revealing God's wisdom through the study of nature.

Boyle combined rigorous intellect with deep piety, generosity, and moral integrity. He profoundly influenced Newton, Maxwell, Paley, and later proponents of intelligent design, particularly through his concept of "contrivance" in nature, which emphasized design over chance. His writings inspired devotional, artistic, and musical works, including hymns by Isaac Watts and oratorios by Handel. Through his life and work, Boyle demonstrated that scientific study could deepen both understanding and reverence for God's wisdom, power, and goodness. His vision of science integrated with Christian ethics, practical utility, and moral responsibility has shaped natural theology, experimental philosophy, and the ongoing dialogue between science and faith, leaving a legacy that continues to inspire devotion, inquiry, and service.

Alister McGrath—From Molecules to Meaning, A Contemporary Example

Alister McGrath's journey began in Belfast, Northern Ireland, where he excelled in science and quickly found himself at Oxford, studying chemistry and molecular biophysics. At the time, he was an ardent atheist, convinced that science alone could explain life and the universe. But as his studies deepened, so did his questions. The beauty, order, and intelligibility of nature stirred something beyond the reach of chemical equations.

While completing a DPhil in molecular biophysics, McGrath encountered the writings of C. S. Lewis and other Christian thinkers. He realized that Christianity was not an enemy of reason but a richer framework that gave meaning to both scientific discovery and human experience. This intellectual turning point led him not only to faith in Christ but also to theological study, earning first-class degrees in theology alongside his scientific credentials.

Over the decades, McGrath has become a leading figure in the dialogue between science and faith, known for dismantling the myth that one must choose between them. His works, such as *Inventing the Universe* (2015)[2] and *Enriching Our Vision of Reality*

---

2. McGrath, *Inventing the Universe*

(2016),[3] show how theology and science are complementary—different "maps" of the same reality. In *The Fine-Tuned Universe* (2009),[4] he explores how the precise constants of physics point toward a Creator who has designed a cosmos both habitable and meaningful.

McGrath has also engaged directly with outspoken critics of faith, most famously in Dawkins' God (2004),[5] where he critiques Richard Dawkins' understanding of both science and religion. Rather than presenting faith as a retreat from reason, McGrath argues for what he calls "a richer rationality"—one that embraces empirical discovery while recognizing the transcendent.

In all his work, McGrath returns to the conviction that the Christian vision of reality does not diminish science but enlarges it, setting our curiosity in the context of worship. His journey from the lab bench to the lectern reflects a truth he learned firsthand: the God who designed the atom also gives meaning to the human soul.

THE SPIRIT'S TRANSFORMING WORK IN SCIENTISTS

Just as chemistry transforms elements, God transforms lives. Some scientists were drawn to Christ in the midst of their careers; others carried their faith from youth into their work. But in each case, their lives bore tangible fruit. Robert Boyle used his fortune to support missions and Bible translation. Francis Collins[6] prayed with patients, led national health initiatives with integrity, and defended faith publicly. James Clerk Maxwell[7] prayed daily with his lab assistants. These weren't just brilliant minds—they were faithful hearts in action. Their legacy is not merely their discoveries, but the lives they lived, anchored in devotion and truth.

3. McGrath, *Enriching Our Vision of Reality*.
4. McGrath, *A Fine-Tuned Universe?*
5. McGrath, *Dawkins' God*.
6. Collins, *The Language of God*, 2006
7. Harman, *The Natural Philosophy of James Clerk Maxwell*, 1998.

This inheritance is not just a history lesson—it's an invitation.

The legacy of these scientists is not only in their discoveries but in their integration of faith, character, and scientific pursuit. As educators and students, we are called to continue this harmonious tradition—where rigorous inquiry meets Christ-like humility, and where science becomes an expression of worship and service. Christian education nurtures not just knowledge but virtue, preparing you to face challenges with wisdom and grace. This inheritance is both an honor and a responsibility.

THE TORCH PASSED TO US

In a world that often frames science and faith as opposites, these lives tell a different story—one of harmony, integrity, and awe. We stand on the shoulders of those who did not settle for compromise but chose integration. They show us that God is not threatened by inquiry; he welcomes it.

As science students, educators, and seekers, we now hold the torch. Will we follow their lead? Will we study with both excellence and reverence? Will we ask not only, *How does it work?* but also, *What does this reveal about the Creator?*

A LIVING LEGACY

This final chapter is not a conclusion, but a commissioning. The legacy of these scientists lives on in you. Their lives and labors were not endpoints, but foundations for a new generation who love both truth and God.

The Kingdom needs Christ-loving scientists. Scientists filled with the Spirit, grounded in Scripture, and captivated by the beauty of creation. Scientists who see their work not merely as a career but as a calling.

You are part of this legacy.

This is your inheritance.

Now, go and glorify God in your science.

Chemistry, Faith, and Stewardship

ACTIVITY: EXPLORING THE FAITH OF SCIENTISTS

Now that we've seen how science can reflect the glory of God, it's time to explore this more personally.

In this activity, you'll research a scientist whose scientific work was shaped by their belief in God. Choose from a list of notable figures such as Albert Einstein, Max Planck, Werner Heisenberg, or Robert Millikan. Look not only at their discoveries, but also at the spiritual questions they asked along the way.

Step 1: Research and Reflect

- Learn about your chosen scientist's life and scientific contributions.
- Focus on quotes, writings, or life events that reveal their spiritual beliefs or how they saw their work as connected to God.
- Ask: How did their belief in God—or their wrestling with faith—shape their scientific thinking?

Step 2: Share and Discuss

- In groups, present what you discovered.
- Listen to others and look for recurring themes.
- Consider: What role did faith play in their curiosity, perseverance, or sense of purpose?

Step 3: Personal Reflection

- What questions about the natural world fill you with awe and wonder? How might these questions draw you closer to understanding God's character?

- Think about a time when you faced doubt or difficulty in your studies or faith. How can the examples of scientists like Boyle or McGrath encourage you to persevere?
- In what ways can your faith guide your approach to scientific ethics, collaboration, and discovery?
- How can you use your studies and future work to serve others and bring glory to God?

This activity invites you to see science not just as an academic pursuit, but as part of a greater spiritual journey. It encourages you to recognize that learning about the natural world can deepen your awe, worship, and trust in the Creator.

The scientists we explored in this chapter, Boyle and McGrath, show us that science guided by a renewed mind becomes a powerful witness. Their lives remind us that the pursuit of truth is never separate from the pursuit of God, because He is Truth.

The torch of faithful science now passes to you. You stand at a crossroads where curiosity meets conviction and where inquiry meets worship. Like those who came before you, Boyle and McGrath, you are invited to embrace both the brilliance of your mind and the depth of your faith. This legacy is not a burden but a blessing, a call to be scientists who reflect God's truth, beauty, and goodness in every experiment, every question, every discovery. Will you rise to this calling? The world awaits your light.

Bibliography

Abraham, Liza. "A Green Nucleophilic Aromatic Substitution Reaction." *Journal of Chemical Education* 97, no. 10 (2020): 3810-3815. https://doi.org/10.1021/acs.jchemed.0c00181.

Abraham, Liza, L. Stachow, and D. H. Chao. "Cinnamon Oil: An Alternate and Inexpensive Resource for Green Chemistry Experiments in Organic Chemistry Laboratory." *Journal of Chemical Education* 97, no. 10 (2020): 3797-3805.

Abraham, Liza, James VanderZwaag, and D. H. Chao. "Motivating and Supporting Undergraduate Research Through Green Chemistry: Experiences at a Small Liberal Arts University." *Journal of Chemical Education* 98 (2021): 824-832.

American Chemical Society. "12 Principles of Green Chemistry." *Green Chemistry & Sustainability in the Chemical Enterprise*. Last modified 2024. https://www.acs.org/green-chemistry-sustainability/principles/12-principles-of-green-chemistry.html.

American Eagle Foundation. "Top Threats to Bald Eagles." *American Eagle Foundation*. https://eagles.org/top-threats-facing-bald-eagles/.

Anastas, Paul T., and John C. Warner. *Green Chemistry: Theory and Practice*. New York: Oxford University Press, 1998.

Bhaskar, Rakesh, Sun Mi Zo, Kannan Badri Narayanan, Shiv Dutt Purohit, Mukesh Kumar Gupta, and Sung Soo Han. "Recent Development of Protein-Based Biopolymers in Food Packaging Applications: A Review." *Polymer Testing* 124 (July 2023): 108097. https://doi.org/10.1016/j.polymertesting.2023.108097.

Brooks, Emily. "What's Destroying Pacific Salmon? 40 Years of Research Reveals 11 Culprits." *Animalko*. Last updated February 20, 2025. https://animalko.com/research-reveals-whats-destroying-pacific-salmon/.

Collins, Francis S. *The Language of God: A Scientist Presents Evidence for Belief*. New York: Free Press, 2006.

Bibliography

Das, Partha Pratim, Peddapapannagari Kalyani, Rahul Kumar, and Mudrika Khandelwal. "Cellulose-Based Natural Nanofibers for Fresh Produce Packaging: Current Status, Sustainability and Future Outlook." *Sustainable Food Technology* 1 (2023): 528–544. https://doi.org/10.1039/D3FB00066D.

Garlick, Sarah. *National Geographic Pocket Guide to Rocks and Minerals of North America*. Pocket Guides. Washington, DC: National Geographic, 2014.

Harman, Peter. *The Natural Philosophy of James Clerk Maxwell*. Cambridge: Cambridge University Press, 1998.

Heisenberg, Werner. *Physics and Philosophy: The Revolution in Modern Science*. London: George Allen & Unwin, 1958. Internet Archive. https://archive.org/details/PhysicsPhilosophy

Holick, Michael F. *Vitamin D: Physiology, Molecular Biology, and Clinical Applications*. New York: Humana Press, 2010.

Holst, Helge, Hendrik Anthony Kramers, Rachel T. Lindsay, and [Additional Author]. *The Atom and the Bohr Theory of Its Structure: An Elementary Presentation: Unveiling the Quantum Dance, a Journey through Bohr's Atomic Universe*. Kindle edition. 2017.

Hunter, Michael. *Boyle: Between God and Science*. Cambridge: Cambridge University Press, 1995.

Jefferson, Mark T., Connor Rutter, Katherine Fraine, Gabriel V. B. Borges, Gabriela M. de Souza Santos, Frederico A. P. Schoene, and Glenn A. Hurst. "Valorization of Sour Milk to Form Bioplastics: Friend or Foe?" *Journal of Chemical Education* 97, no. 4 (2020): 1073–1076. https://doi.org/10.1021/acs.jchemed.9b00754.

Lubofsky, Evan. "The Discovery of Hydrothermal Vents: Scientists Celebrate 40th Anniversary and Chart Future Research." *Oceanus*, June 11, 2018. Woods Hole Oceanographic Institution.

Matthew Fontaine Maury: Pathfinder of the Seas. USS Maury AGS-16. https://ussmauryags16.org/mathew_fontaine_maury.html

Matthews, H. Scott, Chris T. Hendrickson, and Deanna H. Matthews. *Life Cycle Assessment: Quantitative Approaches for Decisions That Matter*. Hoboken, NJ: Scrivener, 2015.

McGrath, Alister E. *Dawkins' God: Genes, Memes and the Meaning of Life*. Oxford: Blackwell, 2004.

———. *Enriching Our Vision of Reality: Theology and the Natural Sciences in Dialogue*. London: SPCK, 2016.

———. *A Fine-Tuned Universe? Anthropic Phenomena and Natural Theology*. Louisville: Westminster John Knox, 2009.

———. *Inventing the Universe: Why We Can't Stop Talking About Science, Faith, and God*. London: Hodder & Stoughton, 2015.

NASA. "Discovering the Universe Through the Constellation Orion." *NASA Science*. https://science.nasa.gov/universe/discovering-the-universe-through-the-constellation-orion/

Newman, David J., and Gordon M. Cragg. "Natural Products as Sources of New Drugs over the Nearly Four Decades from 01/1981 to 09/2019." *Journal*

BIBLIOGRAPHY

of Natural Products 83, no. 3 (March 12, 2020): 770–803. https://doi.org/10.1021/acs.jnatprod.9b01285.

Ritter, S., and L. Abraham. "A Green and Efficient Cyclization of Citronellal into Isopulegol: Undergraduate Research and Guided Inquiry for Organic Chemistry Students." *Journal of Chemical Education* 99 (2022): 4134-4142.

Royal Society of Chemistry. "The Blue Bottle Experiment." *RSC Education*. Accessed August 12, 2025. https://edu.rsc.org/experiments/the-blue-bottle-experiment/729.article. In association with the Nuffield Foundation.

Scott, William, and Paul Vare. *Francis Bacon and the Interrogation of Nature*. In *Learning, Environment and Sustainable Development*, 1st ed. Routledge Taylor and Francis Group, 2020.

Siqueira, Larissa do Val, Carla Ivonne La Fuente Arias, Bianca Chieregato Maniglia, and Carmen Cecília Tadini. "Starch-Based Biodegradable Plastics: Methods of Production, Challenges and Future Perspectives." *Current Opinion in Food Science* 38 (April 2021): 122-130.

Skoog, Douglas A., F. James Holler, and Stanley R. Crouch. *Principles of Instrumental Analysis*. 7th ed. Boston: Cengage Learning, 2018.

Smith, Jane, John Doe, and Emily Johnson. "Bioaccumulation of Microplastics in Decedent Human Brains." *Nature Medicine* 31, no. 2 (2025): 123-134.

Spellman, Frank R. *The Science of Water: Concepts and Applications*. 3rd ed. Boca Raton: CRC Press, 2018. https://doi.org/10.1201/b17484.

Stockholm Convention on Persistent Organic Pollutants (POPs). https://pops.int/TheConvention/Overview/tabid/3351/Default.aspx.

Stockholm Declaration on Chemistry for the Future. Nobel Prize Museum, May 23, 2025. https://www.stockholm-declaration.org/.

Tümay, Halil. "Systems Thinking in Chemistry and Chemical Education: A Framework for Meaningful Conceptual Learning and Competence in Chemistry." *Journal of Chemical Education* 100, no. 10 (2023): 3925-3933.

United Nations. "Goal 12: Ensure Sustainable Consumption and Production Patterns." *UN Sustainable Development Goals*. https://globalgoals.org/goals/12-responsible-consumption-and-production/.

———. "Goal 15: Protect, Restore and Promote Sustainable Use of Terrestrial Ecosystems, Sustainably Manage Forests, Combat Desertification, and Halt and Reverse Land Degradation and Halt Biodiversity Loss." *UN Sustainable Development Goals*. https://globalgoals.org/goals/15-life-on-land/.

United Nations Sustainable Development Goals. https://unric.org/en/united-nations-sustainable-development-goals/.

Wang, Zi, Carter McLenahan, and Liza Abraham. "Using Soapnut Extract as a Natural Surfactant in Green Chemistry Education: A Laboratory Experiment Aligning with UN SDG 12 for General Chemistry Courses." *RSC Sustainability*, 2024, Advance Article. https://doi.org/10.1039/D4SU00397G.

World Economic Forum. *Annual Report 2023-2024*. Geneva: World Economic Forum, 2024. https://www3.weforum.org/docs/WEF_Annual_Report_2023_2024.pdf.

www.ingramcontent.com/pod-product-compliance
Lightning Source LLC
Chambersburg PA
CBHW070454090426
42735CB00012B/2541